From Witchery to Sanctity

Other Titles of Interest from St. Augustine's Press

Winston S. Churchill, *The River War: An Historical Account of the Reconquest of the Soudan* (in two volumes, slipcased)

Winston S. Churchill, *Savrola*

George J. Marlin, *The American Catholic Voter: Two Hundred Years of Political Impact*

Bernard J. O'Connor, *Papal Diplomacy: John Paul II and the Culture of Peace*

E. Michael Jones, *The Slaughter of Cities: Urban Renewal as Ethnic Cleansing*

George A. Kelly, *The Second Spring of the Church in America*

Kenneth D. Whitehead, ed., *The Catholic Imagination*

Kenneth D. Whitehead, ed., *The Catholic Citizen: Debating the Issues of Justice*

Richard Peddicord, S.J., *The Sacred Monster of Thomism: An Introduction to the Life and Legacy of Reginald Garrigou-Lagrange, O.P.*

Michael Davis, *Wonderlust: Ruminations on Liberal Education*

Josef Pieper, *Leisure, the Basis of Culture*

Josef Pieper, *In Tune with the World: A Theory of Festivity*

Roger Scruton, *Perictione in Colophon*

Roger Scruton, *Xanthippic Dialogues*

Roger Scruton, *An Intelligent Person's Guide to Modern Culture*

Ralph McInerny, *The Defamation of Pius XII*

C.S. Lewis and Don Giovanni Calabria, *The Latin Letters of C.S. Lewis*

Florent Gaboriau, *The Conversion of Edith Stein* (translated by Ralph McInerny)

John Lukacs, *Confessions of an Original Sinner*

Jacques Maritain, *Natural Law: Reflections on Theory and Practice*

Marion Montgomery, *Making: The Proper Habit of Our Being*

Marion Montgomery, *Romancing Reality: Homo Viator and the Scandal Called Beauty*

From Witchery to Sanctity
The Religious Vicissitudes of the Hawthornes

Otto Bird and Katharine Bird

St. Augustine's Press
South Bend, Indiana
2005

Manufactured in the United States of America.

1 2 3 4 5   10 09 08 07 06 05

Library of Congress Cataloging in Publication Data
Bird, Otto A., 1914–
    From witchery to sanctity : the religious vicissitudes of the Hawthornes / Otto Bird and Katharine Bird.
     p. cm.
    Includes bibliographical references and index.
    ISBN 1-58731-252-2 (alk. paper)
    1. Hawthorne, Nathaniel, 1804–1864 – Religion.
    2. Religion in literature. 3. Hawthorne, Nathaniel, 1804–1864 – Homes and haunts – Massachusetts – Salem. 4. Hawthorne, Nathaniel, 1804–1864 – Family. 5. Salem (Mass.) – Religious life and customs. 6. Salem (Mass.) – In literature. 7. Salem (Mass.) – Biography. 8. Hawthorne family. I. Bird, Katharine, 1937– II. Title.
PS1892.R4 B57 2003
813'.3 – dc21   2002151653

∞ *The paper used in this publication meets the minimum requirements of the International Organisation for Standardization (ISO) – Paper for documents – Requirements for permanence – ISO 9706: 1994.*

St. Augustine's Press
www.staugustine.net

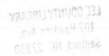

Contents

THE HAWTHORNES

William Hathorne 1606/7–1681
Nathaniel Hawthorne's paternal great-great-great-grandfather

John Hathorne 1641–1717
Hawthorne's paternal great-great-grandfather

Joseph Hathorne 1692–1762
Hawthorne's paternal great-grandfather

Daniel Hathorne 1731–1796
Hawthorne's paternal grandfather

Nathaniel Hathorne 1775/6–1808
Hawthorne's father

Nathaniel Hawthorne 1804–1864

Rose Hawthorne Lathrop 1851–1926
(Mother Alphonsa)
Hawthorne's daughter

Prologue

The glimmering shadows, that lay half asleep between the door of the house and the public highway, were a kind of spiritual medium, seen through which the edifice had not quite the aspect of belonging to the material world. Certainly it had little in common with those ordinary abodes, which stand so imminent upon the road that every passerby can thrust his head, as it were, into the domestic circle. . . . It was the very spot for the residence of a clergyman; a man not estranged from human life, yet enveloped, in the midst of it, with a veil woven of intermingled gloom and brightness. . . . When I first saw the room, its walls were blackened with the smoke of unnumbered years, and made still blacker by the grim prints of Puritan ministers that hung around. These worthies looked strangely like bad angels, or at least like men who had wrestled so continually and so sternly with the devil, that somewhat of his sooty fierceness had been imparted to their own visages. They had all vanished now.

So Nathaniel Hawthorne wrote in introducing his readers to the author residing in the "Old Parsonage" from which he wrote the stories collected in the book titled *Mosses from an Old Manse.*[1] Although the originals of the portraits had vanished from the author, they remained still present not only in the pictures on the wall, but also in the living memory of the writer. He was the descendent in the sixth generation of one of the Puritan founders of Salem, and the Hathornes of the first two generations contributed largely to its religious history. The novelist, writing in the introduction to the *Scarlet Letter*, declared:

> It is now nearly two centuries and a quarter since the orig-
> inal Briton, the earliest emigrant of my name, made his
> appearance in the wild and forest-bordered settlement,
> which has since become a city. And here his descendants
> have been born and died, and have mingled their earthly
> substance with the soil.

Then, of his ancestors reaching back to the first days of the colony, he wrote: "Let them scorn me as they will, strong traits of their nature have intertwined themselves with mine."[2] And here he spoke not only as a family member but also as a writer whose interests and talents were rooted in that history. For the Puritan heritage and its religious concerns provided major sub-ject matter for the novelist and teller of tales.

The words just quoted that the writer applied to himself also hold true of the family as a whole, from its first member in Salem down to the writer and even beyond to his children. It is a story enveloped with "a veil woven of intermingled gloom and brightness."

That history began in America with the arrival in Massachusetts of William Hathorne, who, after a religious con-version, felt that he had been called to help build and support a Puritan church and state in 17th-century Salem. To achieve this purpose he considered it a duty to prosecute persons of other beliefs and even to execute those suspected of witchery.

The 18th century saw a falling away from the strong earnest-ness of the first Puritans and an awakening to the motions of a spirit that led to the rise of Unitarianism. In the 19th century, Nathaniel Hawthorne, although he neither believed nor prac-ticed any organized institutional religion, still wrote tales and novels heavily weighted with problems of sin and guilt and other such religious concerns. The 20th century produced still another variation on the religious theme in Rose Hawthorne Lathrop, youngest child of the writer, who became a Roman Catholic and founded a religious order to care for the destitute dying of cancer. Now, seventy-five years after her death, she is being proposed as a candidate for canonization.

The history of the Hawthornes, more than that of most New England families of the period, focuses on religion. It concerns the vicissitudes of the Christian faith as believed, practiced, and lived by succeeding generations of an extraordinary family.

Endnotes

1   Preface to *Tales*, pp. 1123–25.
2   In *Novels*, pp. 126–27.

Part 1

From Puritanism to Unitarianism

The Puritan Hawthornes

The earliest of the Hawthornes noted historically for the intensity of their religious convictions was the one who became the first Puritan of the family, the emigrant to New England, and one of the first citizens of Salem, Massachusetts. However, the family memory retained the legend of an earlier Hawthorne who had also been struck, and fortunately so, by an inspiration that was taken to be religious. It occurred in the Catholic time before the Protestant Reformation to a Hawthorne who kept an inn and a tavern called The Woodman near the village of Bray in Berkshire on the road between London and Oxford. This innkeeper had a dream in which a beautiful lady appeared to him and told him be at London Bridge upon a certain date. He thought nothing of it until the same lady spoke to him in two more dreams, whereupon he carried out her instructions. At the appointed time he waited on the steps of the chapel on London Bridge. There he fell into conversation with a citizen who, on learning that the innkeeper was acting on message from a dream, dismissed that as nonsense. The citizen added that he knew this from experience since he too had a dream telling him that he would find a treasure if he dug under a tree atop of Hawthorne Hill, a place he had never heard of and would not attempt to look for over all of England. The innkeeper, who had not divulged that he was the owner of Hawthorne Hill, hurried home, dug under the tree, and discovered a pot full of gold coins. For a week he kept his find secret, and then on the night that he brought the pot into the open two clerks of Oxford stopped at the inn for food and rest. They admired the pot, identified the coins as of Roman make, and translated the inscription upon the vessel as saying

> Beneath the place where this pot stood,
> There is another twice as good.

The innkeeper, his wife and servants, and the two clerks mounted the hill, dug more deeply in the same hole and found a second pot twice as full of gold coins. The clerks, who were priests, on being told of the dream, claimed that the vision must have been of the Blessed Virgin herself. The religious innkeeper out of gratitude renamed his inn "The Money Pot," and thereafter gave most generously to the Church.

This legend can be seen to have had later repercussions, or hidden influences. The novelist, Nathaniel, took at least a hint of it for one of his earliest stories, "An Old Woman's Tale," and especially later in his life, became especially attached, if not devoted, to Our Lady, at least in idea and image, and he treasured pictures of her.[1]

So much for the legend.

The first of the Hawthornes known historically to be directed by his religious belief was one William, born at Hawthorne Hill near the village of Bray in Berkshire, England, about 1606. His family, yeomen in origin, by this time had become prosperous. His great-great-grandfather, also a William, in addition to his own farm had acquired though marriage a second farm in Binfield and had leased more land until he controlled 150 acres, become a warden of Bray Church in 1600–1602, married his three daughters well, and married his younger son, the first Nathaniel by name, to an heiress from whom he acquired Staverton Manor as well as the holding of the manor of South Braham in Somersetshire. His older brother, also William, inherited the Binfield farm, was rich, and also opposed to the reform movement at work within the Anglican Church known as Puritanism. His son is the William who commands our attention.

This William is known to have been well educated. Since he turned against the faith of his fathers in favor of the reform doctrines of the Puritans, religion must have carried much weight with him. What then were the principles and beliefs at issue in his religious concerns?

No evidence remains to indicate how the Hawthorne family believed and acted during the violent and often bloody actions that resulted in the establishment of the Church of England as independent of the Roman Catholic Church and subject to the English monarch. William's grandfather (also a William) was born about 1543 and since he served as a warden of the parish church at Bray in 1600–1602 was a member of the Church of England. He also had the reputation of being opposed to the reform movement within the church known as Puritanism.[2]

The basic teachings that constitute the rule of faith of the Church of England are set forth in the Thirty Nine Articles of Religion of 1571.[3] They reveal the influence not only of Roman Catholic teachings of the pre-Tridentine church, but also of Lutheranism and Calvinism. By name the main object attacked and criticized is the Catholic Church. Thus Art. XIX declares, "As the Church of Jerusalem, Alexandria, and Antioch have erred; so also the Church of Rome hath erred, not only in their living and manner of Ceremonies, but also in matters of Faith." The only other community singled out by name is that of the Anabaptists, who are censured for maintaining the common ownership of property (Art. XXXVIII). However, the positive statements of the Articles indicate clearly the principal sources of belief.

Articles I–V and VIII declare the traditional Catholic doctrines regarding the Holy Trinity: "And in the unity of this Godhead there be three Persons, of one substance, power, and eternity; the Father, the Son, and the Holy Ghost." That "the Word or Son of God, which was made very man," born of the blessed Virgin, in the one person on Jesus Christ is of "two whole and perfect natures, who truly suffered, was crucified, dead, and buried, to reconcile his Father to us, and to be a sacrifice, not only for original guilt, but also for actual sins of men." That He descended into Hell, rose again from the dead, and "ascended into Heaven, and there sitteth, until he return to judge all Men at the last day." That "the Holy Ghost, proceeding from the Father and the Son, is of one substance, majesty, and glory, with the Father and the Son, very and eternal God." And that "the Nicene Creed, and that which is commonly called the Apostles' Creed, ought thoroughly to be received and believed."

Articles VI–VII adopt the position of the reform in making Sacred Scripture the sole and sufficient norm for salvation: "so that whatever is not read therein, nor may be proved thereby, is not to be required of any man, that it should be believed as an article of the Faith, or be thought requisite or necessary to salvation." Certain books of the Old Testament accepted as canonical by the Catholic Church were also relegated to the Apocrypha.

Articles IX–XXIV, XXXI–XXXIV, and XXXVI–XXXIX declare teachings that are characteristic of Lutheranism. These concern the corruption of human nature by original sin such that of himself without the faith in Christ he can do no good. Hence justification is only by faith: "We are accounted righteous before God, only for the merits of our Lord and Savior Jesus Christ by Faith, and not for our own works or deserving" (Art. XI). The "Romish Doctrine concerning Purgatory, Pardons, Worshipping, and Adoration, as well as Relics, and also Invocation of Saints" are repudiated as "repugnant to the Word of God" (Art. XXII), as is the use in Church of "a tongue not understood by the people," which amounts to a prohibition of Latin as a liturgical language (Art. XXIV). Transubstantiation, "or the change of the substance of Bread and Wine in the Supper of the Lord," is declared to be "repugnant to the plain words of Scripture . . . and occasion to many superstitions" (Art. XXVIII). The marriage of priests is admitted (Art. XXXII). The rule of Rome over the liturgy is denied: "Every particular or national Church hath authority to ordain, change, and abolish, Ceremonies or Rites of the Church" (Art. XXXIV).

The influence of Calvinism is also behind some of the Articles just mentioned, but it is especially manifest in those on the sacraments and on predestination. The sacraments claimed to be of Christ's own ordination are reduced to two, Baptism and the Supper of the Lord. The remaining five of the traditional seven. Confirmation, Penance, Holy Orders, Matrimony, and Extreme Unction, "are not to be counted for sacraments of the Gospel" (Art. XXV). Article XVII on Predestination and election is especially significant not only for stating the doctrine that some people have been predestined to life eternal "before the foundations of the world were laid; "but also for describing the experimental test by which that election may be known: It is "full of sweet, pleasant, and unspeakable comfort to godly persons, and such as feel in themselves the working of the Spirit of Christ, mortifying the works of the flesh, and their earthly members, and drawing up their mind to high and heavenly things, as well because it doth greatly establish and confirm their faith of eternal salvation to be enjoyed through Christ, as because it doth fervently kindle their love towards God."

If these Thirty Nine Articles of Religion were conceived and expressed in such a way as to be inclusive enough not to alienate the principal Christian worshippers of England, they failed to achieve that purpose. They failed to satisfy at one end the Christians who wanted to remain faithful to Rome and at the other end those who wanted to "purify" their church still more of any taint of Roman Catholicism in either belief or practice. Religious conformity could be obtained only by applying the legal sanctions of the state.

The Puritans, as the purifying party came to be called (the New England divine, Cotton Mather, said it was a nickname)[4] met increasing opposition as Archbishop William Laud became the controlling power within the Church England. Laud whom the novelist described as "the bigoted and haughty half . . . primate."[5] He was determined to enforce strict conformity to the Thirty Nine Articles and the liturgical practices of the Book of Common Prayer. This effort entailed confronting the Puritans directly upon their leading tenets. He defended the position of the episcopacy against the demand for its abolition. The rituals of worship as established had to be followed despite Puritan belief that they were remnants of Roman practice. He called for the end of the lengthy preaching favored by the Puritans as the main task of their ministers, since Laud saw it as a principal source for religious differences. These policies constituted a major threat that had to be met if the Puritans were to maintain their own particular religious beliefs and practices.

One way in which to meet the threat that became increasingly attractive was the way out taken by some of their more radical brethren. They had fled church and state in England by crossing the Atlantic and establishing their own colony as the settlers of Plymouth had done, becoming as they were later called the Pilgrim fathers. It was with members of a group in Dorchester favoring such a course of action that William Hathorne became associated.

Evidence is not now available of the reasons the young Hathorne may have had for siding with the Puritan party, even when his father opposed them, a split in the family foreshadowing another in the 19th-century Hawthorne family in Massachusetts. He is known to have been in Dorchester, where he may have heard the influential preaching of the Rev. John White, who as known as the Patriarch of Dorchester, and who strongly advocated leaving England for America and was himself a member of the group in the town preparing to establish a plantation in Massachusetts.[6] According to Puritan teaching, the principal and indeed indispensable requirement was a deeply felt experience of conversion: a powerful all but overwhelming conviction of being visited by the Holy Spirit and assured of salvation in and by the Lord through the gift of divine grace. In this the teaching differed strongly from the traditional Catholic doctrine. For St. Augustine as well as for St. Thomas, no person could know that he or she was in a state of supernatural grace, and it was a presumptuous temptation to think so.[7] William evidently experienced such a conversion. He was welcomed by the Puritan group and accepted as a member of the group that would establish the Massachusetts Bay Colony. His brother-in-law and friend Richard Davenport was one of the earliest members.

The expense of outfitting, transporting, and establishing a plantation, as it was called, was met by forming a joint-stock company. For this a patent was obtained from the government, and men willing to venture funds in the enterprise came forward. The patentees who invested £50 were promised 200 acres of land for their first dividend. Neither Hathorne nor Davenport was among the investors, although John Endicott, the future governor was. The following year in 1629 a royal charter was granted which recognized the company and drew up its governing body as consisting of a governor, deputy, and eighteen assistants to be elected by the freeman of the company, thereby, in effect, granting the right of self-government to the colony.[8] It was the Massachusetts Bay Company so established and chartered that William Hathorne joined and became one of the group going to America to establish a new plantation.

The Puritans setting out for the new world went at least partly, if not principally, for reasons of religion. But not all those doing so went with the express purpose of erecting a new church separate from the Church of England. Of the 102 founders of the colony of Plymouth only 35 were acknowledged Separatists, consisting of those who had fled to Leyden or in the Netherlands. The remaining sixty seven aboard the *Mayflower* were faithful to the Church of England and hired to protect the interests of the joint-stock company. The colonists for Massachusetts Bay on leaving England in 1630 were told by John Winthrop, their governor, that "the principals, and body of our company . . . esteem it our honor to call the *Church of*

England, from whence we rise, our dear Mother . . . we leave it not therefore, as loathing that milk wherewith we were nourished there, but blessing God for the parentage and education, as members of the same body, shall always rejoice in her good."[9]

However, once they crossed Atlantic and reached their destination the way that the new colonists began to organize their church and practice its worship presented little evidence of fidelity to the Church of England, or at least to its practices as set down in the Book of Common Prayer. Thus the church at Salem is said to have begun when "thirty persons entered into a covenant in writing . . . and that the ministers were ordained or instituted anew." Two of the company who were among the first patentees objected to this departure from Anglican practice and withdrew to form a separate society, thus protesting against what they considered outright non-conformity. For their own non-conformity to the new order of the settlers, they were ejected from the colony and sent back to England.[10]

Yet the new settlers of Massachusetts Bay, however they failed to conform to Anglican practice, did not declare themselves Separatists, as the colonists at Plymouth had. They considered themselves as belonging to the Church of England but desirous of further purifying it. They also refused to ally themselves with the Puritans who had adopted the Presbyterian form of church organization. They no more wanted their church to be ruled by presbyters than they wanted bishops. Theirs was the Congregational ideal.

The Congregational plan of church government seems to have first obtained that name from the Rev. John Cotton when he came to the colony in 1633. The simplest statement of that platform, as it was called, distinguishes four characteristics as follows:

> 1st. The subject matter of the visible church, viz. saints by calling, such as are acquainted with the principles of religion, and who profess their faith, and the manner how they were brought to the knowledge of God by faith in Christ,

either viva voce, or else by a public declaration thereof made by the elders, as it has been delivered to them in private; although if such profession be scandalized by an unchristian conversation, it is not to be regarded.

2d. The constitutive part of a particular visible church ought to be, a restipulation or mutual covenanting, to walk together in their Christian communion, according to the rule of the gospel.

3d. No church ought to be of larger extent or greater number than may ordinarily meet together in one place, for the enjoyment of all the same numerical ordinances and celebrating all divine worship, nor fewer, ordinarily, than conveniently may carry on church work.

4th. That there is no jurisdiction to which particular churches are or ought to be subject, by way of authoritative censure, nor any other church power, extrinsical to such churches, which they ought to depend upon any other sort of men for the exercise of.[11]

The essential principle making such an organization "congregational" consists in the way it is conceived to exist: Each gathering forms a congregation that establishes a church that is independent, autonomous, and separate from all other churches, regardless of how established, even from those following the same congregational platform. Thus in the first days of the colony even the associating of the ministers of the various churches was frowned upon. The assertion of autonomous jurisdiction implicit in the form or organization and stated explicitly in the 4th article denies and abrogates the episcopacy and any subjection to the office of bishop.

The other principles declared in the platform shared by other Puritan groups included that: membership depends upon a conversional experience such as to certify a "saint"; only individuals so certified, as it were, qualify to come together and "covenant" or agree to live and worship together; the rule by which they will regulate their actions is provided by the Bible.

Such was the doctrine of the church of which William Hathorne became a member and indeed helped to establish, protect, and promote on coming to Massachusetts. He arrived from England in 1630 accompanied by his sister, Elizabeth, who was soon married to Richard Davenport, and perhaps his younger brother also came with them. William settled at Naumkeag, which was soon renamed Salem, and soon became one of the leaders of the settlement. By 1634 he had been administered the oath, making him a freeman, declared a member in good standing of the church, and elected a member of the General Court, the legislative and executive organ of the colony, a body that he was to serve in several offices throughout his life. In 1637 he was granted 200 acres of land in Salem Village and there upon named the neighboring land Hawthorne Hill, perhaps in memory of his ancestral origin in England.

There are three areas in which the activities of Hathorne bear upon the religious concerns of the Puritan: military, ecclesiastical, and legal or judicial.

The military situation arose from the fact that the new settlers were occupying a land already claimed and dwelt in by others, the American Indians. Hence from their arrival the colonists had to prepare themselves to protect themselves from the Indians even at the risk of war. Militias were accordingly formed in the various plantations. In that of Salem Hathorne became a leading officer. In 1644 he was made a Captain and years later a Major and led attacks upon the Indian forces.

However, apart from the question of defense, the relation of the settlers to the Indians also raised a moral issue. This question regarded the rightness of the colonists settling upon land taken from the Indians. The Rev. Francis Higginson, who became minister of the First Church in Salem, before leaving England in 1629, had written a promotional defense of the New England settlements, titled "General Considerations for the Plantation in New England, with an answer to several objections." Among the objections that he raised was the following: "But what warrant have we to take that land, which is and hath been of long tyme possessed by others, the sons of Adam?" To this he answered that the land in question was common to all and proper to none; that it had not been enclosed and put to use, but lay waste and so could be taken as "lawfully as Abraham did among the Sodomites"; that no civil right had been acquired for the land such as "the right which Ephron, the Hittite, had to the field of Machpelab, wherein Abraham could not bury a dead corpse without leave"; and lastly that "there is more land than is sufficient for both the Indians and colonists."[12]

The same objection was made again by Roger Williams when he arrived to become a minister to the church of Salem. Williams, taken by a later century as an apostle of religious freedom, was a thorn of contention in Massachusetts Bay. Not only for raising embarrassing questions such as this concerning Indian land, but also because of innovations he wanted to introduce in religious observances. In 1635, he was arraigned before the General Court among other acts for administering oaths to the impenitent, holding that no one should pray with impenitent persons, even though that person be his own wife or child, demanding that women should wear veils when they appeared in public, and finally that it was unchristian for the flag of the king and so of the militia to bear the sign of the cross.[13]

This last proposal found favor in Salem, even with the leader of its militia, John Endicott, frequently governor. Endicott drew up the militia formed into a hollow square, demanded that the standard-bearer lower the flag, and then with his own sword he cut out the cross from the flag. For this act he was later reprimanded before the General Court. The incident also provided the novelist with the material for a story celebrating defiance against both pope and tyrant, entitled "Endicott and the Red Cross."

William Hathorne is known to have been a good member of the church and certified as such, since otherwise he could not have qualified to hold public office. The other qualifications were being a freeman, at least twenty-four years of age, a property owner, and not a factious, litigious spirit – all that Hathorne also met.[14] He was evidently a leader in the First Church. There is a report of an ordination of a minister in which he addressed the congregation on their responsibilities in such a procedure, obtained their consent, and then with two deacons accomplished the ordination by laying their hands upon the chosen person.[15] Presumably in the eyes of his church, he won greatest credit in acting as a guardian of morals, for which he won the reputation of being the most dreaded person in Essex County.[16] This fame, if not honor, he obtained primarily for his work as trial judge and director of the police, an office he held for thirteen years. This activity can be accounted as much as a work for the church as for the state because of the extremely close relation between the two in the early colony. This relation was described by one minister thus:

> Church government and civil government may very well stand together, it being the duty of the magistrate to take care of matters of religion, and to improve his civil authority for observing the duties commanded in the first as well as the second table [of the Ten Commandments], seeing the end of their office is not only the quiet and peaceable life of the subject in matters of righteousness and honesty, but also in matters of godliness. I Tim.ii.1,2.[17]

Because of this close relation the public official was expected to oversee the morals of the citizenry and punish those who failed to observe them. It was his duty to punish drunkenness, swearing, immodesty, violation of the sexual code, disrespect of governing or religious officials, failure to attend religious service, non-conformity to the belief and practice of the church, as well as any actions deemed to deserve capital punishment. These latter were specified in the first code of laws drawn up by the colony in the "Body of Liberties," as follows:

> I. If any man after legal conviction shall have or worship any other God but the Lord God, he shall be put to death (Deut. 13:6,10; Deut. 17:2,6 Ex. 22:21).

II. If any man or woman be a witch (that is, has or consults with a familiar spirit), they shall be put to death (Ex. 22:18; Lev. 20:27; Deut. 18:10).

III. If any person shall blaspheme the name of God the Father, Son, or Holy Ghost, with direct, express, presumptuous, or high-handed blasphemy, or shall curse God in the like manner, he shall be put to death (Lev. 24:15–16).

IV. If any person commit any willful murder, which is manslaughter, committed upon premeditated malice, hatred, or cruelty, not in a man's necessary and just defense, nor by mere casualty against his will, he shall be put to death (Ex. 21:12; Num. 35:13; 14:30–31).

V. If any person slay another suddenly in his anger or cruelty of passion, he shall be put to death (Num. 25:20–1; Lev. 24:17)

VI. If any person shall slay another through guile, either by poisoning or other such devilish practice, he shall be put to death (Ex. 21:14)

VII. If any man or woman shall lie with any beast or brute creature by carnal copulation, they shall surely be put to death. And the beast shall be slain, and buried, and not eaten. (Lev. 20:15–16).

VIII. If any man lies with mankind as he lies with a woman, both of them have committed abomination, they both shall surely be put to death (Lev. 20:13).

IX. If any person commits adultery with a married or espoused wife, the adulterer and adulteress shall surely be put to death (Lev. 20:19 and 18:20; Deut. 22:23–24).

X. If any man steals a man or mankind, he shall surely be put to death (Ex. 21:16).

XI. If any man rise up by false witness, wittingly and of purpose to take away any man's life, he shall be put to death (Deut. 19:16, 18–19).

XII. If any man shall conspire and attempt any invasion,
insurrection, or public rebellion against our Common-
wealth, or shall endeavor to surprise any town or towns,
fort or forts therein, or shall treacherously and perfidiously
attempt the alteration and subversion of our frame of poli-
ty or government fundamentally, he shall be put to death.[18]

As can be noted, the Puritan framers of these capital laws
were careful to note the warrant in Scripture for each of
them, except for the last one.

Major Hathorne does not appear to have been at all lax in
meeting his official responsibilities for the morals of Salem.
Court records indicate that he exacted punishment for crimes
such as drunkenness, swearing, and fornication. He is also
noted as taking the lead in the prosecution of the Quakers who
began arriving in Salem in 1657 and criticizing the Christianity
of the First Church. Protests of the Quakers at time took extreme
forms. Thus one Quaker wife was brought to court for running
naked through town "as a sign of spiritual nakedness in town,"
and sentenced to being tied to the end of a cart, stripped to the
waist, and whipped "not exceeding thirty stripes."[19]

The novelist, Nathaniel, in a long story entitled "The Gentle
Boy," describes the cruel effects the prosecution of Quaker par-
ents has upon their orphaned boy and the difficulties a kind
Puritan met in trying to befriend him.

Major Hathorne throughout his long life frequently filled
government offices. He was a Representative from 1636–43;
Speaker part of 1644 and again in 1646; Deputy in 1649; Speaker
again in 1650; Deputy in 1651, 1652, and 1656; Speaker in 1657;
Deputy in 1658–59; and Speaker in 1660 and 1661.[20]

A scandalous case of interest to later Hawthornes came to
court in 1680 when Captain Nicholas Manning was charged
with incest with his two sisters. He was judged guilty but fled
successfully; the sisters were fined; and his wife, who brought
the charges, obtained a divorce. Over a century later in 1801 the

Nicholas's descendant Elizabeth Clarke Manning married Captain Nathaniel Hathorne, the parents of the novelist.[21]

William Hathorne in addition to his many official duties proved also to be a successful farmer and businessman. In 1663 he married his eldest son to Abigail Corwin, daughter of Salem's richest man, and turned over his business dealings to that son. He died in 1681, old, famous, and rich, leaving an estate of £750, a considerable sum for that time. For this first Puritan ancestor, the novelist has provided a portrait in words along with a comment on the ancestor's influence on him:

> The figure of that first ancestor, invested by family tradition with a dim and dusty grandeur, was present to my boyish imagination, as far back as I can remember. It still haunts me, and induces a sort of home-feeling with the past, which I scarcely claim in reference to the present phase of the town. I seem to have a stronger claim to a residence here on account of this grave, bearded, sable-cloaked and steeple crowned progenitor, – who came so early with his Bible and his sword, and trode the unworn street with such a stately port and made so large a figure, as a man of war and peace, – a stronger claim than for myself, whose is seldome heard and my face hardly known. He was a soldier, legislator, judge, he was a ruler in the Church, he had all the Puritanic traits, both good and evil. He was, likewise, a bitter perse-cutor; as witness the Quaker, who have remembered him in their histories, and relate an incident of his hard severity towards a woman of their sect, which will last longer, it is to be feared, than any record of his better deeds, although these were many.[22]

Endnotes

1   Vernon Loggins, *The Hawthornes: The Story of the Seven Generations of an American Family* (New York: Columbia University Press, 1951), pp. 3–11.

2   *Ibid.*, pp. 12–13.

3   *The Book of Common Prayer* (New York. Oxford University Press, 1929), pp. 591–98.

4   Cotton Mather, "Life of John Eliot," *Magnalia Christi Americana*, Book III in Perry Miller and T. H. Johnson, *The Puritans* vol. II (New York: Harper & Row, 1963), p. 499.

5   "Endicott and the Red Cross" in *Tales and Sketches* (The Library of America, 1982), p. 542.

6   Loggins, p. 16–18.

7   St. Thomas Aquinas, *Summa Theologica*, I-II.5,c.

8   Thomas Hutchinson, *The History of the Colony and Province of Massachusetts Bay*, edited by L. S. Mayo, vol. I (Cambridge, Mass.: Harvard University Press, 1936), pp. 10–18.

9   *Ibid.*, I, 408.

10   *Ibid.*, I, 12–13.

11   *Ibid*, I, 354–55.

12   Joseph B. Felt, *Annals of Salem*, vol. I (W & S B Ives, 1845), pp. 69, 72–73.

13   *Ibid.*, II, 571.

14   *Ibid.*, I, 353, 357.

15   Hutchinson, I, p. 359.

16   Loggins, p. 41.

17   Hutchinson, I, 366.

18   *Mass. Hist. Soc. Collec.* VIII, pp. 216–37.

19   Loggins, pp. 58–63.

20   *Ibid.*, pp. 88–89, 198.

21   Felt, II, p. 564.

22   *The Scarlet Letter*, "Introductory," from *Novels* (The Library of America, 1983), p. 126.

The Witch Trial Judge

Hawthorne the writer took great interest in the history of Puritan Massachusetts, and especially of his native town of Salem. He had carefully studied its records, and these provided him with much material for his writings. The sketch entitled "Main-street" describes "characteristic scenes that have passed along this thoroughfare [of Salem] during more than two centuries of its existence . . . the ghosts of his forefathers, amid a succession of historic incidents."[1] Among the many scenes presented, Hawthorne pays special attention to the victims and persecutors in the witchcraft trials of late 17th-century Salem, describing their persons and the charges brought against them. The author obviously was fascinated as well as horrified by the madness over witchery. The lore surrounding, it as well as the historical persons engaged in it, frequently occur in his writings. Hawthorne's interest was more than artistic in furnishing material for his writings. In addition, the material was intensely personal, since one of the leading agents in the famous trials of 1692 was his own ancestor, John Hathorne.

John, the most infamous of the Hawthornes, was the eldest son of Major William Hathorne.[2] He was born in Salem August 4, 1641, and received his first schooling there in the institution established by the "Old Deluder Law" of 1647. This law called for the establishment of a school for reading and writing in each town containing at least 50 households and beyond that in towns with 100 households a school to prepare boys for entering the university. The law got its name from its purpose of combating Satan, the Old Deluder, in his attempts to keep people from knowledge of the Sacred Scriptures. The boy John received his first schooling from the institution established in Salem in accord with that law.

When John was in his teen years he was voted a member of the First Church and thereafter remained a faithful practicing member of that church. Although faithful and a strong upholder of the same views his father had about the relation of church and state, he was brought up in the Puritan faith and not a new convert to it as his father was. He attended the long Sunday services that began at nine in the morning with the singing of Psalms, followed by a long prayer and a longer sermon until 1 pm, and then resumed an hour later for more of the same until evening.

In his career John also followed that of his father and devoted his talents and energy to farming, business, military service in the wars against the Indians, and political and legal activity as a judge and member holding various offices in town government and the General Court of the colony. But he devoted more of his time to business than his father had. He kept accounting for various merchants, engaged in occasional sea voyages and ventured capital in them, and eventually possessed a wharf of his own. In 1666 he acquired the Robin Hood tract in Maine, amounting to about 9,000 acres, that constituted the "eastern land" that later and poorer Hawthornes would fondly dream of as a source of wealth. John was evidently the most prosperous of the Hawthornes.

His first public office came in 1674 when he was appointed deputy marshal. After serving in the Indian wars he was made town clerk in 1679 and four years later became deputy of the General Court and the next year in 1684 Assistant, thereby acquiring all the privileges in government of the colony that his father had held. With the end of the Puritan government in England and the reestablishment of the monarchy and of the Anglican Church in England, the Massachusetts Bay Colony also came to the end of the Puritan monopoly of power there. John Hathorne stood with the conservative Puritans in opposing the efforts of the crown to reassert its own control. He fought to hold on to the old order in which he had been born and brought up, including religious uniformity and purity, theocratic rule, the death penalty for heresy, restriction of the franchise to free men, and prohibition of the use of the Book of Common Prayer in church services. For this opposition he was cited in 1686 for disloyalty and ordered to appear for arraignment in London. This eventuality he managed to avoid by stalling until in 1688 the "Glorious Revolution" removed James II from the throne, and then John took part in the action of overthrowing that king's governor in Massachusetts. In 1691, a new charter was imposed upon the colony, making it a province, and ending theocratic rule. But stirring, exciting, and upsetting as such events had been, greater were still to follow the very next year. For in 1692 the witchcraft trials came to their climax.

Witchcraft was then considered one of the deadliest of sins and the worst of crimes. The Body of Liberties, as we have seen, places it second only to the failure to believe and worship the one true God and before blasphemy, murder, sodomy, bestiality, adultery, theft, false witness, and rebellion. Nor was this belief unique to 17th-century Massachusetts. As William Blackstone, the great authority on English Common Law, wrote in the 1760s, "witchcraft, conjuration, enchantment, or sorcery . . . is a truth to which every nation in the world hath in its turn borne testimony, either by examples seemingly well attested or by prohibitory laws; which at least suppose the possibility of commerce with evil spirits."[3]

Trials and execution for witchcraft had also occurred in Massachusetts prior to 1692. In 1648 Margaret Jones of Charleston had been hanged as a witch; in Boston 1656 Ms. Ann Hibbins (whose name the novelist appropriated for a witch in *The Scarlet Letter*) met a similar fate;[4] and in the 1680s Mary Glover, a Roman Catholic from Ireland was found guilty and executed for bewitching four children of the Godwin family in Boston. But although there had been precedents in these trials, it was not until 1692 that the search for witches and the prosecution of them became a mania that threatened to reach epidemic proportions. Beginning in January and lasting until September of that year in Salem twenty persons and two dogs were accused, tried, found guilty of witchcraft, and executed; 150 persons were in jail awaiting trial on that charge; and 200 more had been accused of the same crime.[5]

The trouble began in Salem Village (now Danvers), some five miles north of Salem. The Rev. Samuel Parris was minister of the church there, a position that he had held since 1688. Before that he had been a merchant in Barbados, and from there he had brought two slaves of mixed Indian and Negro blood, John and his wife Tituba. The Parris family included two young girls, nine-year-old daughter Elizabeth, and an eleven-year-old niece, Abigail Williams. Tituba, evidently as a way of amusing the children, showed off her skill in magic in which she would pretend to be someone else. The children were so delighted that they soon imitated her and let loose their fancies, so much so that Abigail began to claim in her tricks that she ceased to be herself and became a different person. They played without trouble until she fell sick, as did Elizabeth and other play-mates. A doctor was called in, but he could find nothing wrong, whereupon he came up with the diagnosis that proved fateful: witchcraft, he claimed, caused the children's illness.

The questions that Judge Hathorne addressed to the accused suspects provide clues to the effects that 17th-century people believed witchcraft was capable of producing. But before considering those investigations, we should note the basic principles underlying the trials. The first is that God can, has, and does intervene in the affairs of the world and of humankind, and that Satan does likewise. New England was thought to be especially subject to such visitations. The Rev. Cotton Mather, head of the church in Boston, and author of *Memorable Providences Relation to Witchcraft and Possessions* (1689), a writing that contributed greatly to the furor over witches, put it this way:

> The New Englanders are a people of God settled in those, which were once the devil's territories. . . . I believe that never were more satanical devices used for the unsettling of any people under the sun than what have been employed for the extirpation of the vine which God has here planted. . . . Wherefore, the devil is now making one attempt more upon us; an attempt more difficult, more surprising, more snarled with unintelligible circumstances than any that we have hitherto encountered . . . a horrible plot against the country by witchcraft, and a foundation of witchcraft then laid, which if it were not seasonably discovered would probably blow up and pull down all the churches in the country.[6]

And as already noted, it was believed that if the church falls it brings the state and government down with it.

But justification for the trials, in addition to belief in the existence and operation of Satan in the world, required the further principle that Satan could work out his purposes only through the agency of human beings. For this reason Satan's work could only be discovered and thwarted by finding and identifying his human agent, namely the witch. Sharing such beliefs, the judges confronted with an accusation of witchcraft were prepared to undertake an investigation to discover the guilty one. John Hathorne was such a judge.

However, a judge could not be called in until an accusation was made. In the Parris case, the identity of a person to be accused was found by calling in the help of an expert in the science of demons. Before this the Rev. Parris had sought advice from several ministers in the neighborhood who were knowledgeable in books on the subject. However, when they tried to put their book knowledge into practice by asking the sick girls,

"Who is hurting you?" the only answer they got was in the form of a fit. The expert then called in was a neighbor, Goody Mary Sibley.

"Goody" was the shortened form of address of Goodman or Goodwoman in the colony for those who did not merit the title of Master or Misses, the latter two being reserved for those who were gentlemen, members of the three professions, schoolmasters, military and sea captains, college graduates with two degrees, and freemen, and their wives.

Goody Sibley prescribed a rite that John, Tituba's husband, performed. He mixed together rye meal with the children's urine to make a cake that then was baked in the kitchen hearth. The cake was fed to the dog and then the children responded to the leading question. At first they said only that it was Tituba who was hurting them. But later they named two more women, Sarah Good and Sarah Osburn, both poor and living on the outskirts of the town. These three supplied the necessary accused, and they were summoned to appear before John Hathorne and Jonathan Corwin to answer charges of being witches and harming the girls of the Parris family and their friends.

The judges were prepared to follow the procedures of investigation believed capable of revealing the presence of a witch and of obtaining a confession. These procedures included attempting to trick the accused into admitting that she had made a pact with Satan, had engaged in Satanic mysteries that mocked baptism and communion, and had made ghostly visits to those she had harmed. In addition, the accused person was forced to undergo an examination since, according to the beliefs of the day, witches usually bore witch marks on their bodies in the form of unnatural excrescences and marks of suckling demons. Also the possessions of the accused were searched for such items as puppets and dolls made out of hair and rags to resemble the victim. Extraordinary feats and displays of unusual strength such as no normal person could perform were also taken as evidence of demonic possession and power.

The first of the preliminary hearings in the Parris case was held in Salem Village meeting house March 1, 1692. All three of the accused were questioned that first day, Tituba much the longest. Goody Good was the first of these. After unsuccessful attempts to trick her into a confession of guilt, Hathorne had her meet the ill children, but they could not stand before her eyes, fell into "fits," and uttered strange screams. Goody Good denied that she was the cause and attributed it to Goody Osburn, although this person was not present then in the meeting house. Good's husband was said to believe that his wife was a witch, but he testified that he had never seen a mark of Satan on his wife's body, although her treatment of him had shown that she was "an enemy to all virtue."

Goody Osburn received a still shorter examination. Judge Hathorne again commanded the children to look at her, and again they suffered the same contortions as before, showing that they were all "hurt" afflicted, and tortured very much." Hathorne, by his repeated questioning, got her to admit that "she was frightened one time in her sleep and either saw or dreamed that she was a thing like an Indian, all black, which did prick her in her neck, and pull her by the back part of her head to the door of the house." The poor frail old lady was also made to agree that the Devil might have visited the children, dressed in her likeness.

Tituba was examined at much greater length than either of the other two. She was no sooner brought into the meetinghouse than the children began to scream and writhe as though in pain. Asked directly by Hawthorne why she so hurt the children, Tituba replied, "They do no harm to me. I no hurt them." She denied knowing "when the Devil works" or that he told her anything, and yet acknowledged that the Devil might be hurting them at that time. Asked about his appearance, she said that he was "Like a man, I think," and went on to declare that "one night in the lean-to chamber at my master's house I see a thing like a man. He tell me to serve him, and I tell him that I do no such thing. It's Goody Osburn and Goody Good that hurt the children. They come to me one night while I was the room, and the man he with them, and two other women. They tell me to hurt the children too. They say if I no do, they hurt me. Then I obey, but after I do I tell them I do so no more."

Under further questioning Tituba said that the Devil did not always appear as a man, but that she had seen him as a hog, a large black dog, and with him she had also seen a little yellow bird, two cats, one red, the other black and as big as a dog, who had scratched her, although she denied that she had given them suck. She also claimed that the two other women he forced her to go with them, and the three had ridden upon a stick to the house of Ann Putnam with the intent of killing the child. At this remark the child Ann Putnam interrupted to say that Good and Osburn had appeared to her and ordered her to "cut off your own head," and that if she did not, Tituba would. According to Tituba, Good was accompanied by the yellow bird the man had given her, while Osburn had two things: "One hath wings and two legs, and a head like a woman. The children see it one day, and before their eyes it turn into a woman. Osburn hath also a thing all hairy, with two legs. It goeth upright like a man, and one night it stand before the fire in my master's hall."

Tituba provided still further descriptions. The Devil, appearing in the likeness of a man, had white hair and was dressed in black, although at other times in still different clothes. The two other women whom she had mentioned but could not identify were described, one as wearing a black silk hood with a white silk one beneath it and also topknots, the other as a smaller wearing a serge coat and a white cap. Hearing this, the children in the case fell unconscious again into violent contortions, and on coming to agreed with Tituba that it was Goody Good who was hurting them. One of the girls then fell into an even more violent fit and on regaining consciousness said that she had several torturers whom she did not know because they had blinded her.

So ended the first day of the preliminary hearings into the Parris case held by Mr. Hathorne and Mr. Corwin.

The next day, March 2nd, the hearings continued, and again Tituba was the main respondent. The frail Osburn woman was questioned first, but she admitted nothing and accused no one. Tituba, however, although refusing to say that she had made any pact with Satan, did admit that she had dealings with him. According to her testimony, "the man" had come to her before Abigail got sick, read to her from a book, and said he would let her look into the book if she promised to serve him for six years. He then left, but soon returned, showed her the book, and got her to make her mark in it "with red, like blood." She saw other names in the book, nine in all, some red, some yellow, two of which the Devil said were those of Good and Osburn. As Tituba made her mark, she reported that the Devil said to her: "Serve me! And serve me always"

After the two days of hearings, it was agreed that the evidence was sufficient to warrant holding them and committing them for trial. But there was unfinished business still remaining. Tituba at the first hearing had referred to two unknown women and on the second day had seen in the Devil's book seven marks in addition to those of Good and Osburn. Hathorne and Corwin were determined to do what they could to establish the identity of these others, and to that end held two more hearings on March 3rd and 5th, both without success. Then on March 7th they issued orders for the jailing in Boston of Sarah Good, Sarah Osburn, and Tituba Indian.

The triumph of Hathorne and Corwin in their efforts to uncover the work of the Devil was celebrated by both church and state. On March 19th in the meeting house that had been the scene of their success, the Rev. Deodate Lawson, friend of Cotton Mather and the predecessor of Mr. Parris in the Salem Village Church, lauded the two magistrates in a sermon. The approbation of the state came on April 11th when several more persons accused by the sick children were to be examined. For this purpose the hearings were moved to the more spacious quarters that Salem afforded and conducted by superior officials who came from Boston, including the Deputy Governor Thomas Danforth, and the chief justice in Massachusetts Samuel Sewall.

Magical practices were not limited to the witches. Hathorne himself is said to have resorted to magic in order to achieve an identification. Some of the afflicted that he was examining were unable to point out a man accused of witchcraft. Hathorne then moved the hearing into the yard outside the meeting house and had a large circle drawn upon the ground. On its completion a girl who was in a trance at once called out: "There's John Alden, a bold fellow, with his hat on before the judges! He sells powder and shot to the Indians, and lies with the Indian squaws, and has papooses!" This man, who was then committed, was an old successful Boston merchant. (Alden was the son of the John Alden immortalized for his courting of Priscilla Mullins in early Plymouth when he sent Captain Miles Standish to ask for her hand in marriage. Her famous response was, "Why don't you speak for yourself, John?"[7]) The Alden jailed on suspicion of being a witch succeeded in breaking jail and so avoiding trial.

After the investigation of the Parris case, Hathorne and Corwin continued to hold preliminary hearings of persons accused of witchcraft. Frequently the hearings were held in the Corwin house, which led to it becoming known later as the "witch house." The two men were also among the nine magistrates named by the governor to try the accused and call for the execution of those found guilty. But there is no record that Hathorne ever sat at the trials. Between June and the middle of October he had examined and committed as many as a hundred suspects, and thus may have been too busy for any other duties. Yet he did witness the execution of those condemned by the trial court, many if not all of whom he had examined and committed. The calendar of the principal hangings that Hathorne as magistrate presided over probably reads as follows:

June 10, the first execution was that of Bridget Bishop, tavern keeper, who in 1680 had been sentenced to hang as a witch but then had been pardoned by the governor. The hangings took place at Gallows Hill, as it later came to be known, not far from the Mill Pond farm that the Hawthornes' owned.

June 19, five women were hanged, including Sarah Good, who uttered a curse long remembered in the Hawthorne family. Just before her hanging, the Rev. Nicholas Noyes screamed at her: "You're a witch, and you know you are." To whom Goody Good cried back: "You're a liar! I'm no more a witch than you're a wizard! And if you take my life God will give you blood to drink!" Later historians attributed this curse to Rebecca Nurse, also hanged this day, and addressed not to Noyes but to Hathorne. The curse is the one that the novelist used as the source of the troubles in *The House of Seven Gables*.[8]

August 19, four men and one woman were executed, including the Rev. George Burroughs and Martha Carrier of Andover. The man had been formerly the minister at Salem Village, but unable to pacify the contentious parish, he had returned to his former home in Wells, Maine, to minister to its church. Those claiming to be afflicted by him claimed that the ghost of two former wives had testified that Burroughs had murdered them. His execution was attended also by the two eminent Puritan divines, Increase and Cotton Mather. About to be hanged, Burroughs repeated the Lord's Prayer so movingly as to bring tears to some of the witnesses. One of the indications of being a witch was supposedly the inability to say correctly the Lord's Prayer.

At the hanging of Martha Carrier, Cotton Mather cried out: "This is the hag whom the Devil promised to make the Queen of Hell." She came from Andover where the witch trouble was almost as great as at Salem. Three of her children, one a girl of eight years, testified that their mother, in the form of a cat, had threatened to kill them unless they signed Satan's book. It was also at Andover that a dog was tried and executed on the charge of bewitching people.

September 19, Giles Corey died. Because he refused to say any word, and thus submit to trial, he was condemned not to hanging but to "pressing," i.e., to having stone after stone piled upon his chest until he died. It took three days to kill the eighty-year-old man. Later he was celebrated in a ballad which had the refrain, "'More weight! More weight' / Giles Corey he cried."

September 22, eight women were hanged, including Corey's wife Martha. The comment of the Rev. Noyes was: "What a sad thing it is to see eight firebrands of hell hanging there."

That date marked the end of executions for witchcraft in Salem. Since that date of September 22, 1692, no one has been executed as a witch in Massachusetts.

The new governor, Sir William Phipps, saw that the mania over witchcraft that was seizing the land had to be stopped. By the following spring of 1693 he had granted reprieves for those awaiting execution and the release of those under arrest. Among those given freedom was Tituba. She had been kept under arrest but not executed, presumably on the assumption that she might identify more suspects. Her master, the Rev. Parris, refused to pay the charges for her keep in jail, and she was sold. But before she disappeared from history, she several times told others that she had been forced by Mr. Parris to give the account that she had to Mr. Hathorne and that proved to be start of the witchcraft scare in Salem.

In 1694 Parris himself is said to have made "a Christian-like acknowledgement to some brethren of his church, dissatisfied with the part he had taken," and its council the following year advised that if he were unable to continue at Salem Village he could leave with their recommendation.[9]

The life of John Hathorne did not end with the last of the witch trials and executions, although that marked the conclusion of his greatest days of fame, or infamy. He lived to receive further honors from both state and church. In 1702 he was made judge of the superior court of the province, and he was upon several times to represent the church of Salem at the synods that were convened. In 1712, at the age of seventy one, he retired as judge and died five years later, having lived and officiated in several offices during the ruling days of the Puritans in Massachusetts Bay.[10]

His descendant in the 19th century, the novelist, must have pondered over the mania about witches and wizards, for he remarked upon not only the responsibility of his ancestor, the judge, for the cruelties committed, but also about the shame that he himself yet felt. This is what the novelist said in an autobiographical note in the introduction to *The Scarlet Letter*, about his ancestor, the witch trial judge: He

> inherited the persecuting spirit, and made himself so conspicuous in the martyrdom of the witches, that their blood may fairly be said to have left a stain upon him. So deep a stain, indeed, that his old dry bones, in the Chester Street burial-ground, must still retain it, if they have not crumbled utterly to dust! I know not whether those ancestors of mine bethought themselves to repent and ask pardon of Heaven for their cruelties; or whether they are now groaning under the heavy consequences of them, in another state of being. At all events, I, the present writer, as their representative, hereby take shame upon myself for their sakes, and pray that any curse incurred by them – as I have heard, and as the drearly and unprosperous condition of the race, for many a long year back, would argue to exist – may be now and henceforth removed.[11]

Endnotes

1   "Main Street" in *Tales and Sketches* (The Library of America, 1982), p. 1023.

2   The account of John Hathorne's life and activities, especially that of the witch trials, is drawn almost entirely from the chapter entitled "Witchcraft, Alas" from Vernon Loggins, *The Hawthornes: The Story of Seven Generations of an American Family* (New York: Columbia University Press, 1951), pp. 114–41.

3   William Blackstone, *Commentaries on the Laws of English*, edited by George Sharswood, 2 vols. (Philadelphia: J. B. Lippincott & Co., 1872), IV.4.vi.60.

4   *Scarlet Letter* in *Novels* (The Library of America, 1983), p. 217.

5   E. H. Miller, *Salem Is My Dwelling: A Life of Nathaniel Hawthorne* (Iowa City: Iowa University Press, 1991), p. 735.

6   Cotton Mather, *The Wonders of the Invisible World* (London, 1862), pp. 9–10.

7   H. W., Longfellow, "Courtship of Miles Standish," in *The Complete Poetical Works*, vol. III (Boston: Houghton-Mifflin Company, undated), conclusion.

8   *House of Seven Gables* in *Novels*, p. 358.

9.   Joseph B. Felt, *Annals of Salem*, 2 vols. (W & S B Ives, 1845), II, p. 484.

10. *Ibid.*, I, p. 166.

11   *Scarlet Letter* in *Novels*, pp. 126–27.

The Puritan Relapse to Unitarianism

Hawthorne in the historical sketch entitled "Main Street" observed that the faith of the first Puritan settlers failed to retain its original intensity:

> All was well, so long as their lamps were freshly kindled at the heavenly flame. After a while, however, whether in their time or their children's, these lamps began to burn more dimly, or with a less genuine luster.[1]

The dimming or relaxing of that faith became evident among the Hawthorne family. Judge William Hathorne, the persecutor of Quakers, had the reputation of being the most dreaded person in Essex County. His son John, although fanatical in his hunting of witches, was not as strongly conservative in his religious beliefs, and even took for his wife a woman those mother had once been a Quaker.[2] The third generation of the American Hawthornes witnessed the first break-up of the original Congregational Church in Salem. In 1718 some 40–50 members of that church withdrew their allegiance in order to set up their own church, known as the East Church while the original one became the First Church. Among this group were Jacob Manning, ancestor of the novelist's mother, and Philip English, whose descendants also intermarried with Hawthornes. East Church became the earliest in Salem to welcome Unitarianism.[3] Later in the 1730s still another group seceded and set up a third congregation as the "Tabernacle" Church. About the same time a still-more-violent break from Puritanism occurred when

Manning and English accepted the faith and practice of the Church of England and organized the church and parish of St. Peter's in Salem.[4]

Although Joseph Hathorne was a strong supporter of the old First Church, he could not prevent his sons from abandoning it. Two of his sons married women belonging to the Church of England and adopted the faith of their wives. The youngest son, Daniel, grandfather of the novelist, remained in the First Church, in which he was married. His daughter Rachel, to the dismay of her family, married an Irishman, Simon Forrester, born a Roman Catholic, but who had turned Protestant.[5] The younger son, Nathaniel, father of the writer, in 1801 in the First Church married Elizabeth Clarke Manning, who was related to the Manning who had turned Anglican.[6] She had been regularly worshipping with her parents at the East Church, where she would have heard the liberalizing sermons of its pastor, Rev. William Bentley. There in 1795 the English minister William Hazlitt, father of the essayist, espoused for the first time in Salem the doctrine of Unitarianism. Elizabeth Manning Hawthorne was married in the First Church, which she then continued to attend. Her three children were all baptized there" Elizabeth and Nathaniel in 1806 and Louisa in 1808.[7]

The religious history of the Hawthorne family, even from so brief a sketch, mirrors the vicissitudes that the faith of the Puritans underwent during the course of the 18th century. However, nothing has been said at all about the religious beliefs that lay behind and motivated such changes in religious allegiance. Because of the bearing they have upon Hawthorne's writings and what they can contribute to the understanding of them, especially as they concern religion, it is worth investigating at least the major issues of the controversy.

The Congregational Way of worship and church government achieved its fullest development with the adoption of the Cambridge Platform in 1648. It enunciated a religious plan of life that was clear, definite, rigorous, and detailed. Especially important were the conditions laid down for full membership in the church. In addition to "Repentance from Sin, and faith in Jesus Christ," a person also had to attest to having had a personal experience of conversion and so to "covenant," whereupon he could partake of the Lord's Supper. The baptism of infants could be administered only to those whose parents were full members of the church.

This provision tying together church membership of the parents and baptism of their children came to arouse strong opposition, especially among the second generation of Puritans. Many of the baptized never went on to accomplish their full covenanting and testifying to a conversion experience. They were thus known as only halfway church members, and yet they still demanded that their children be baptized. Ultimately, in 1622 a Synod in Boston's First Church acquiesced by adopting the "Half-Way Covenant."[8]

The issue regarding baptism is one of church discipline, and the decision on 1662 marked an important step in relaxing the original Puritan standards. Still weightier and more significant changes came once basic doctrines of Christian belief began to be criticized and denied. Of these one of the most important was the doctrine of original sin and the innate depravity of human nature. The early Puritan understanding of it was formulated by the Rev. John Davenport (1597–1669), the first minister of New Haven:

> That in as much as Adam was the root of all mankind, the Law and Covenant of works was given to him, as to a publike person, and to an head from whence all good or evil was to be derived to his posterity. Seeing therefore that . . . first Eve, then Adam being seduced did wittingly and willingly fall into the disobedience of the Commandment of God; Death came upon all justly, and reigned over all, yea, over Infants also which have not sinned after the like manner of the transgression of Adam: Hence also it is, that all since the fall of Adam, are begotten in his own likeness, after his Image, being conceived and born in iniquity, and

> so by nature children of wrath, dead in trespasses and sins, altogether filthy and polluted throughout in soule and body; utterly averse from any spiritual good, strongly bent to all evil, and subject to all calamities due to sin in this world and for ever.[9]

Strong support for criticism of the doctrine by Congregational ministers in New England came from a book by the English dissenter of Norwich, John Taylor (1694–1761), entitled *The Scripture-Doctrine of Original Sin* (1740). It controverted the doctrine regarding the natural state of human kind and its ability while denying that Scripture provided any basis for it. According to his interpretation, the only results of sin were sorrow, labor, and mortality, and the last of these was hardly evil since it was countered by the resurrection of Christ. Nor could the guilt of sin be inherited, since sin could only result from a free and evil choice by the individual directly involved. He denied any innate depravity in being a child, declaring that "we are born neither righteous nor sinful; but capable of being either, as we improve or neglect the Goodness of God."[10]

These arguments of Taylor were approved and circulated in New England by the Rev. Charles Chauncy (1705–1787) of the First Church and the Rev. Jonathan Mayhew (1720–66) of the West Church, both in Boston. As their preaching and writing succeeded in persuading others to repudiate the doctrine of original sin and its inheritance, their efforts resulted in further departures from the beliefs of the first Puritans and a lessening of their severity. The subject of sin was also one of great interest to Hawthorne the writer, as we will see when we reach a discussion of his works, and especially of the *House of Seven Gables*.

The denial of original sin and the inheritance of it was a hard blow against orthodox Puritan belief. But the killing blow came with the denial of the divinity of Jesus Christ and the turn to Unitarianism.

The orthodox belief, as stated in the creed of John Davenport, was:

That God is a Spirit most holy, immutable, eternal, every way infinite, in greatness, goodness, power, wisdom, justice, truth, and in all divine perfections. . . . And that in this Godhead, all three distinct persons, coeternall, coeguall, and coessential, being every one of them one and the same God, not three Gods, and therefore not divided in essence, nature or being . . . but distinguished one from another, by their several and peculiar relative property; the Father is of none but of himself, the Son is begotten of the Father before all worlds, the Holy Ghost proceedeth from the Father and the Son, from all eternity, all together are to be worshiped and glorified. . . . That the Lord Jesus, of whom Moses and the Prophets wrote, and whom the Apostles preached, is as touching his person, the everlasting Son of God the Father, by eternall generation, coessential, coequal, and coeternall, God with him, and with the Holy Ghost; by whom he made the world, and by whom he upholdeth and governs all the works he hath made: who also, when the fullness of time was come, was made of a woman, of the Tribe of Judah, of the seed of David and Abraham, viz. of Mary, the Blessed Virgin, by the Holy Ghost coming upon her, and the power of the most high overshadowing her; and was in all things like unto us, sin only excepted; so that in the person of Christ, the two natures, the divine and humane, are truly, perfectly, indivisibly, and distinctly united.[11]

Differences and opposition had been growing within the members of the Congregational Church, both clerical and lay, but it was not until the beginning of the 19th century that they came fully into the open and led to an outright break. One of the first signs of it came with the appointment of a new holder of the Hollis Chair of divinity at Harvard College. Until 1803 it had been safe for orthodoxy, but in that year upon the death of its former occupant, the Rev. Henry Ware (1764–1845), liberal minister of the church in Hingham, was elected to the chair.

A few years later the Orthodox party forced into the open the issues dividing the contending parties. For that purpose they seized upon the *Memoirs* of the father of Unitarianism in

England, Theophilus Lindsey (1723–1808), published by Thomas Belsham in 1812. This book contained a chapter devoted to "American Unitarianism," which quoted letters from prominent New Englanders and claimed that "Most of our Boston Clergy and respectable laymen (of whom we have man enlightened theologians) are Unitarian."[12] This chapter was published as a pamphlet in Boston in 1815 with a preface accusing the "Unitarians" and challenging them to defend themselves.

That the reformist group did by choosing as their spokesman Rev. William E. Channing, minister of the Federal Street Church. His response only widened the breach between the two groups, and any reconciliation became beyond hope when Channing in 1819 preached in Baltimore his most famous sermon, which has been called the *magna carta* of American Unitarianism. The doctrines enunciated in it are of particular relevance to our inquiry since he was known personally to Hawthorne, especially through his sister-in-law Elizabeth Peabody, a devoted follower of Channing and for a time his personal secretary.

We need consider only those teachings that mark the clearest departures from orthodox Puritanism.

On the unity of God:

In the first place, we believe in the doctrine of GOD'S UNITY, or that there is one God, and one only. To this truth we give infinite importance. . . . We understand by it, that there is one being, one mind, one person, one intelligent agent, and only to whom underived and infinite perfection and dominion belong. . . . We find no intimation . . . that God's unity was a quite different thing from the oneness of other intelligent beings.[13]

On the trinity:

We object to the doctrine of the trinity, that whilst acknowledging in words, it subverts in effect, the unity of God. According to this doctrine, there are three infinite and equal persons, possessing supreme divinity. . . . Here then we have three intelligent agents, possessed of different consciousnesses, different wills, and different relations; and if these things do not imply and constitute three minds or beings we are utterly at a loss to know how three minds or beings are to be formed.[14]

On Jesus Christ:
We believe that Jesus is one mind, one soul, one being, as truly one as we are, and equally distinct from the one God. We complain of the doctrine of the trinity, that not satisfied with making God three beings, it makes Jesus Christ two beings, and thus introduces infinite confusion into our conception of his character.[15]

On original sin and guilt:
Orthodoxy teaches that God brings us into life totally deprived, so that under the innocent features of our childhood, is hidden a nature averse to all good and pretense to all evil, a nature, which exposes us to God's displeasure and wrath, even before we have acquired power to understand our duties, or to reflect upon our actions. . . . Now according to the plainest principles of morality, we maintain, that a natural constitution of the mind, unfailingly disposing it to evil and to evil alone, would absolve it from guilt; that to give existence under this condition would argue unspeakable cruelty, and that to punish the sin of this unhappily constituted child with endless ruin, would be a wrong unparalleled by the most merciless despotism."[16]

Channing's Baltimore sermon was followed by a long and bitter controversy among the Congregationalists which resulted in a rupture and the formation of a new denomination. The liberalizing group among them in 1825 formed the American Unitarian Association, which was joined by 125 churches, 100 in Massachusetts alone, including all in Boston with the exception Old South Church.

Hawthorne in 1825 was 21 years old and newly graduated from Bowdoin College. Since this college was a Congregational one, modeled upon Harvard, with a curriculum based chiefly on religion as well as the classical languages and literature, it was unlikely that it could completely escape the religious controversies that we have just described. Yet it is another question whether his college years they had any influence upon the future writer, or whether he paid any attention to them. However, what is known and well documented in his writings is that religious concerns of the Puritans provided him with subjects and themes that excited his imagination and led to his tales and novels.

Endnotes

1   "Main Street," in *Tales and Sketches* (The Library of America, 1982), p. 1031.

2   Vernon Loggins, *The Hawthornes: The Story of Seven Generations of an American Family* (New York: Columbia University Press, 1951), p. 102.

3   *Ibid.*, p. 152.

4   *Ibid.*, pp. 88, 140, 162.

5   *Ibid.*, pp. 162–64.

6   *Ibid.*, pp. 175, 180.

7   *Ibid.*, pp. 191, 198–99, 203.

8   H. Shelton Smith, Robert T. Handy, and Lefferts A. Loetscher, eds., *American Christianity: An Historical Interpretation with Representative Documents*, 2 vols. (New York: Charles Scribner's Sons, 1960), vol. I, pp. 202–3.

9   *Ibid.*, I, p. 109.

10 *Ibid.*, I, p. 380.

11 *Ibid.*, I, pp. 108–9.

12 *Ibid.*, I, p. 483.

13 *Ibid.*, I, p. 495.

14 *Ibid.*

15 *Ibid.*, I, p. 496

16 *Ibid.*, I, pp. 498, 499.

Part 2
Religion in the Writings of Hawthorne

On Institutionalized Religion

Religion is an important and significant subject in the tales and novels of Hawthorne. This is scarcely surprising inasmuch as the early history of Puritan New England supplied the main matter of his work, and that society in its foundation and first centuries was profoundly religious. Yet, as has been frequently pointed out by his critics, Hawthorne the writer showed little interest in theological doctrines and controversies. *The House of the Seven Gables* offers a major exception to this claim, as will be argued at some length in the next chapter. But generally it is true that the interest to the writer lay in the beliefs and practices of religion and their effects upon character. He is much concerned with their darker manifestations as in the writings that deal with deviltry and witchcraft, and, more centrally, the problem of evil and sin in the human world. Many of the characters in the tales and novels evince belief in basic doctrines of the Christian faith, such as in the existence and providence of God, the value of prayer, the distinction between soul and body, the desire for immortality, and the worth of good and godly action and of its reward in heaven. There are also a number of instances in which religion and the issues it poses come to the fore. Some of these deal explicitly with religious leaders; others are critical of the actions to which religion gives rise; still others blame the religions themselves, as in attacks directed against Puritanism or Catholicism.

This last class of subjects in which religion as such is at issue is the principal concern of this chapter. The writings themselves in the tales and novels supply all the evidence, and no attempt will be made to claim that it presents the beliefs of Hawthorne the man. What is said and quoted are the words, beliefs, and opinions of the characters of the stories or even of the narrator, without implying that the narrator in and of the story is Hawthorne the man. It should also be noted in anticipation of the following chapter that our major consideration of religion in the writings will center upon the problem of sin and its consequences as dealt with especially in the three great novels.

On Puritanism

Hawthorne praises the early Puritans, the first white settlers on the land, for their energy and work and chiefly for the plainness of their worship as contrasted with the gorgeous ritual they had known in the great cathedrals of England. The meeting-house occupied the central point in their lives, and of it is written:

> A meaner temple was never consecrated to the worship of the Deity. . . . Their house of worship, like their ceremonial, was naked, simple, and severe. But the zeal of a recovered faith burned like a lamp within their hearts, enriching every thing around them with its radiance; making of these new walls, and this narrow compass, its own cathedral; and being, in itself, that spiritual mystery and experience, of which sacred architecture, pictured windows, and the organ's grand solemnity, are remote and imperfect symbols.[1]

However, not all the early leaders receive such praise, but instead are criticized for the evil they wrought. Among these one of the most prominent is the Puritan divine, Cotton Mather, chief instigator of the furious war against witchcraft. Hawthorne describes Mather as being present among the victims he sent to their execution:

> In the rear of the procession rode a figure on horseback, so darkly conspicuous, so sternly triumphant, that my hearers

mistook him for the visible presence of the fiend himself; but it was only his good friend, Cotton Mather, proud of his well won dignity, as the representative of all the hateful features of his time; the one blood-thirsty man, in whom were concentrated those vices of spirit and errors of opinion, that sufficed to madden the whole surrounding multitude.[2]

Hawthorne's criticism of the ferocity of Puritan religion is not limited only to its treatment of witchery, but is extended to the attacks it directed against any who dared to disagree with any of its tenets. Belief in and adherence to a different religion brought persecution as fierce as that against witches. The Quakers were its object in the early days of the colony, as already noted. In fact, among the Quakers themselves, "the place of greatest uneasiness and peril, and therefore in their eyes the most eligible, was the province of Massachusetts Bay."[3] The tale from which the statement comes tells the pathetic and touching story of the suffering of a Quaker boy named Ilbrahim in a Puritan colony. His father had been executed for his beliefs, his mother banished. Found lying on his father's grave, he was taken in by a kind couple, all of whose children had died. They themselves are then spurned and taunted for harboring a Quaker, and the boy, although beautiful and gentle, causes greater antipathy by rejecting neighbors' efforts to persuade him to adopt the Puritan faith. The three attend a Sunday meeting where they have to hear a two-hour tirade by the minister against the Quakers and the evil of associating or sympathizing with them. A muffled figure of a woman then stood forth, revealing herself to be the mother of Ilbrahim, and she berated with malignant fanaticism the Puritan persecution of the Quakers. Her boy offered to go with her, even into prison, but she refused him with the claim that she had more important work to do. Rejected by his natural mother, he rejoined his adopted parents. Attempting to join a group of children, he was rushed upon and became "the center of a brood of baby-fiends . . . [who] displayed an instinct of destruction, far more loathsome than the blood-thirstiness of manhood."[4] Ilbrahim was badly injured, and although he recovered physically, in spirit he was never the same and began a slow decline. When his Quaker mother eventually returned to the village, she found him dying, and he died in her arms. For a time she continued upon her self-imposed mission, even more fanatic than before. But at length, as though depleted of her wrath, she returned to dwell with her boy's adopted parents:

> As if Ilbrahim's sweetness yet lingered round his ashes; as if his gentle spirit came down from heaven to teach his parent a true religion, her fierce and vindictive nature was softened by the same griefs which had once irritated it.[5]

The story entitled "Endicott and the Red Cross" indicates that the Anglican Church from which the Puritans had fled in coming to Massachusetts could arouse their ire as much as the Quakers did. John Endicott, a founder of Salem and one-time governor of the colony, rose up in anger against even a symbolic display of the hated Anglican religion, and he did so in the name of his Puritan religion. The incident occurred when the royal forces, in an assertion of their authority, attempted to unfurl the English banner with the Red Cross in its field over a company of Puritan militia. Endicott refused to allow it and denounced it as evidence that the English crown aimed "to establish the idolatrous forms of English Episcopacy," which could lead to the erection of "a cross on the spire of this tabernacle which we have builded." He demanded that the flag be lowered, and then with his sword he cut out and threw aside the detested red cross that it bore, boasting that the ensign of New England declared that "Neither Pope nor Tyrant hath part in it now."[6]

Roman Catholicism also comes under attack, especially in *The Marble Faun*, in which the action occurs in Rome and Italy at the time of the Papal States. Hawthorne described the place as being priest-ridden and criticized it for being so, since the clergy is rarely, if ever, presented in a favorable light. Monks and their life always appear as the very image of corruption. When the principal character, who is both Catholic and Italian, announced that he was thinking of entering a monastery, his American Protestant friend angrily rebuked him:

> Then think of it no more, for Heaven's sake! . . . There are a thousand better and more poignant methods of being miserable than that, . . . A monk – I judge from their sensual physiognomies, which meet me at every turn – is inevitably a beast! Their souls, if they have any to begin with, perish out of them, before their sluggish swinish existence is half-done. . . . They serve neither God nor man, and themselves least of all, though their motives be utterly selfish.[7]

When the same character feared that the woman he loved may have turned Catholic, he could not prevent himself from bursting out: "Hilda, have you flung your angelic purity into that mass of unspeakable corruption, the Roman Church?"[8]

Yet in certain respects Hawthorne highly praises the Church and its practices. The Virgin Mary is described as the beautiful image of the divine womanhood and maternity.[9] St. Peter's Basilica is hailed as "the World's Cathedral, as well as that of the palace of the world's Chief-Priest . . . the grandest edifice ever built by man."[10] Little is written about Catholic religious practices with the exception of confession, which is highly commended for the help and relief it can bring to a troubled conscience, but this is a subject to be dealt more fully with in the next chapter. The character Hilda who experienced the relief confession could bring had gone to St. Peter's "to observe how closely and comfortingly the Popish faith applied itself to all human occasion."[11] About that faith the narrator wrote:

> To do it justice, Catholicism is such a miracle of fitness for its own ends, (many of which might seem to be admirable ones,) that it is difficult to imagine it a contrivance of mere man. Its mighty machinery was forged and put together,

not on middle earth, but either above or below. If there were
but angels to work it, (instead of the very different class of
engineers who now manage its cranks and safety-valves,)
the system would soon vindicate the dignity and holiness
of its origin.[12]

The Puritans found another object to direct their ire against
in the person of Anne Hutchinson, one of their own. The sketch
of her life presents her as "a woman of extraordinary talent and
strong imagination" who was prompted by the enthusiasm of
the times "to stand forth as a reformer of religion"[13] Called
before the Synod, the first in New England, she was charged
with heresy. Speaking eloquently in her own defense, she in
effect condemned herself:

> She claims for herself the peculiar power of distinguishing
> between the chosen of man and the Sealed of Heaven, and
> affirms that her gifted eye can see the glory round the fore-
> heads of the Saints, sojourning in their mortal state. She
> declares herself commissioned to separate the true shep-
> herds from the false, and denounces present and future
> judgements on the land, if she be disturbed in her celestial
> errand.[14]

The Synod, concluding she was disturbed, excommunicated
her and banished her from the Massachusetts colony. The narrator noted that this was "a most remarkable case, in which religious freedom was wholly inconsistent with public safety, and
where the principles of an illiberal age indicated the very course
which must have been pursued by worldly policy and enlightened wisdom."[15] Mrs. Hutchinson fled first to Rhode Island,
becoming one of the founders of that state, and then, dissenting
from the religion she found there, she went to Long Island and
"became herself the virtual head, civil and ecclesiastical of a little colony."[16]

Endicott, that "Puritan of Puritans," not only tore out and
demolished the Red Cross in the flag of England, he also

bragged of destroying the only May-Pole in New England. This event occurred when he led a band of militant Puritans against the colony of Merry Mount, now known as Wollaston, Mass. Some of the settlers had transported with them the hereditary games and joyful celebrations they had known in the old country. This was especially true at Merry Mount, where they continued their English tradition: crowned the King of Christmas, elected a Lord of Misrule, and danced the night through around the bonfires lighted on the eve of St. John. But of all their merriment the foremost was their veneration for the May-Pole, decked with flowers and boughs and tended with masks, music, and dancing.

Such revelry was highly obnoxious to the Puritan settlement nearby. Puritans claimed that when a psalm was being sung from their meeting-place, its echo "seemed often like the chorus of a jolly catch, closing with a roar of laughter," surely the work of the fiend and his bond-slaves at Merry Mount. The Puritans were determined to eradicate the evil. They appeared at the end of the last day of mirth around the May-Pole, forcibly halted the merrymaking, while Endicott stood forth, denounced their iniquity, and with his sword demolished the hated May-Pole. With that he declared that "by its fall, is shadowed forth the fate of light and idle mirth-makers, amongst us and our posterity."[17]

In commenting upon the significance of the feud, the narrator wrote:

> The future complexion of New England was involved in this important quarrel. Should the grisly saints establish their jurisdiction over the gay sinners, then would their spirits darken all the clime, and make it a land of clouded visages, of hard toil, of sermon and psalm, forever. But should the banner-staff of Merry Mount be fortunate, sunshine would break upon the hills, and flowers would beautify the forest, and late posterity do homage to the May-Pole![18]

On Mistaken Reform

The story entitled "The Hall of Fantasy" describes a museum devoted to the images of people from every age who have been "rulers and demi-gods in the realms of the imagination." It includes poets and writers, inventors of fantastic machines, speculators on the Exchange, and generally anyone with some "crochet of the brain." among those selected for prominent mention are the "noted reformers of the day, whether in physics, politics, morals, or religion," and it is noted that "there is no surer method of arriving at The Hall of Fantasy than to throw oneself into the current of a theory."[19]

> It would be endless to describe the herd of real or self-styled reformers, that peopled this place of refuge. . . . Many of them had got a possession of some crystal fragment of truth, the brightness of which so dazzled them, that they could see nothing else in the wide universe. Here were men, whose faith embodied itself in the form of a potato; and others whose long beards had a deep spiritual significance. Here was the abolitionist, brandishing his one idea like an iron flail. In a word, there were a thousand shapes of good and evil, faith and infidelity, wisdom and nonsense, – a most incongruous throng.[20]

But there is one theory, it is claimed, that "swallows up and annihilates all others. It is that the good, Old Father Miller, earnest, honest, strongly convinced of his doctrine that "the destruction of the world was close at hand," and "with one puff of his relentless theory" scatters all other dreams "like so many withered leaves upon the blast."[21]

Hawthorne does not repudiate all reform as such. He acknowledges that even the most foolish reform may well be inspired by and contribute to "the struggle of the race after a better and purer life than had yet been realized on earth."[22] Rather it is the fanaticism of a reform based on a single overriding idea as providing a panacea for all woes.

"The Celestial Rail-road," which is a parody of Bunyan's *Pilgrim's Progress*, satirizes the belief that Christian life would be improved if only it were made easier and more comfortable. The parallels with the pilgrimage described by Bunyan, and the changes from it, are explicitly commented upon. The narrator, being near the City of Destruction, learns that a railroad has been established between that flourishing town and the Celestial City and decides to make the trip. He finds himself in the company of a director of the railroad and one of its largest stockholders, named Mr. Smooth-it-away, who assumed the role of guide. They reached the Slough of Despond, into which the Pilgrim, Christian, had fallen and almost sunk, but found that a flimsy bridge had been erected over it that had for its piers books of morality – Plato, Confucius, and Hindu sages – that had converted into a granite-like mass. That which had former-ly been the Wicket Gate, the strait and narrow way to salvation, had become a Station House where tickets were obtained for the train from a suspicious character claiming to be Evangelist. Instead of the poor old Christian of the former pilgrimage, a crowd of prosperous, jolly folk conversed about everything except religion. Nor were they compelled to carry their baggage as a burden on their back, as Christian had to, since attendants now assumed the care of it. Apollyon, the destroying angel of the bottomless pit with whom Christian had fought a fierce bat-tle in the Valley of Humiliation, now functioned as the chief engineer of the train, which "shows the liberality of the age" and proves that "all musty prejudices are in a fair way to be obliter-ated."[23] The interpreter's House, where Christian had received his first extensive instruction on the way to the City, was aban-doned as a way-station, since the keeper of the house was so violently opposed to the building of the rail-road. The Hill of Difficulty, which Christian had to climb with great effort, was penetrated by a great tunnel, the extracted material from which was used to fill the Valley of Humiliation, thus greatly alleviating the passage. The charming ladies Prudence, Piety, and Charity, with whom Christian had passed a pleasant and enlightening time, were now old maids and no longer visited by travelers. The railroad through the Valley of the Shadow of Death had much reduced the terror of the way through it, although it continued to be filled with smoke and murky light. The cave where the cruel giants, Pope and Pagan, had once dwelt, was now occupied by the German called Giant Transcendentalist, the chief peculiarity of whom was that neither he nor anyone else could describe "his form, his features, his substance, and his nature generally."[24] At the flourishing city of Vanity Fair the train made a considerable stop, where Christian and his friend Faithful were seized, tormented, put on trial, and sentenced to death. The new pilgrim found, however, that harmony now reigned between the townspeople and visitors. It was also now filled with churches and many clergy, among the latter mentioned by name were the Rev. Mr. Shallowdeep, the Rev. Mr. Stumble-at-Truth, the Rev. Mr. Bewilderment, the Rev. Mr. Clog-the-Spirit, and greatest of all, the Rev. Mr. Kind-of-doctrine.[25] Outside the city of Vanity lay the castle once owned by the redoubted giant Despair, but upon his death Mr. Flimsy-faith had taken it over and turned it into a house of entertainment. Within sight of the Delectable Mountains the train passed a cavern which Christian had been told was a byway to hell, but Mr. Smooth-it-away claimed that was a lie, since it was no more than a smokehouse. Arrived at the river across which lay the Celestial City, the new pilgrim was surprised that the guide was to leave them, and as he did so the smoke breathed from his mouth and flame from his eyes revealed that Mr. Smooth-it-away was "The Impudent Fiend."[26]

The strongest and most extensive criticism of reform and of the evil that may infest the single-minded reformer with an *idée fixe* is contained in *The Blithedale Romance*. Although it is not directed at organized religion, and hence lies outside our concern, it deserves notice for its analysis of sin, which is the subject of the next chapter.

The central and major theme of the romance is the portrait it draws of a philanthropic utopian attempt at social reform and the effect upon the participants in the effort. Hawthorne himself invested in and lived for a time in the experiment at Brook Farm under Margaret Fuller, and he could not persuade his critics that his novel was not about that community. In a letter he indicates that his primary reason for joining is to check out its suitability as a home for him and his eventual wife, Sophia Peabody. But in a short time Hawthorne left the community, noting in disgust that he found it impossible to labor as a field hand by day and as an intellectual at night. Yet that matter is none of ours, and for our purposes it is sufficient to note the fault and sin of the leader that underlies the failure at Blithedale.

Hollingsworth, the strong leader of the Blithedale community, was well acquainted with the various schemes for social reform that were advocated in his time. Of these he was most strongly opposed to the establishment of cooperative communities such as proposed by Charles Fourier in France. Hollingsworth was disgusted with that theory and repudiated it as vitiated by its basic principle: "I never will forgive this fellow," he declared.

> He has committed the Unpardonable Sin! For what more monstrous iniquity could the Devil himself contrive, than to choose the selfish principle – the principle of all human wrong, the very blackness of man's heart, the portion of ourselves which we shudder at, and which it is the whole aim of spiritual discipline to eradicate – to choose it as the masterworkman of the system.[27]

Yet when the working of the community began to falter, relations between its members to worsen so that tempers began to rise and to burst, it is the sin of self that Hollingsworth is accused of. Zenobia, the leading woman and financial supporter of the experiment, breaks with him and charges him with intense bitterness:

> It is all self! . . . Nothing else, nothing but self, self, self! The fiend, I doubt not, has made his choicest mirth of you these seven years past. . . . You have embodied yourself in a project. You are a better masquerader than the witches and gypsies yonder; for your disguise is self-deception.[28]

The narrator, Miles Coverdale, a bachelor, writer, and member of the Blithedale community, made explicit, as he wrote, the "moral" of the experience:

> That, admitting what is called Philanthropy, when adopted as a profession, to be often useful by its energetic impulse to society at large, it is perilous to the individual, whose ruling passion, in one exclusive channel, it thus becomes. It ruins, or is fearfully apt to ruin, the heart; the rich juices of which God never meant should be pressed violently out, and distilled into alcoholic liquor, by unnatural process; but should render life sweet, bland, and gently beneficent, and insensibly influence other hearts and other lives to the same blessed end. I see in Hollingsworth an exemplification of the most awful truth in Bunyan's book of such; from the very gate of heaven, there is a by-way to the pit.[29]

Conclusion

Religion, except in this last instance, provides the principle motivation for action in the writings that we have just considered. Hawthorne the writer's attitude toward it has been expressed through the words and observations made by the various narrators. Merely in the few tales and sketches analyzed here, these are many and not always in agreement with one another.

Except for *The Blithedale Romance* the narrator is unnamed, and yet even so is often presented as different persons. In the sketches and tales about the early Puritans the narrator appears as an historian; in the "Hall of Fantasy" as a visitor to the hall;

in the "Celestial Rail-road" as a passenger on the train; in *The Marble Faun* as an American Protestant in Rome and Italy. Only in the story of Blithedale does the narrator appear as a character named Miles Coverdale engaged in action with other members of the community.

Yet even when the narrator is an unnamed and supposedly objective historian, the judgment made about religion varies from one writing to another. The action of the Puritans is in effect condemned as unfeeling, cruel, and intolerant in its treatment of the Quakers and their gentle boy; and the mighty Cotton Mather is called a friend of the Fiend, if not the Fiend himself. Yet the illiberal condemnation of Mrs. Hutchinson is explained, if not defended, as politically necessary at the time when the existence of the society depended upon unity of religious belief. So too Endicott's action in rending the Red Cross from the flag is hailed as "one of the boldest exploits which our history records" as "the first omen of that deliverance which our fathers consummated, after the bones of the stern Puritan had lain more than a century in the dust."[30] Yet the judgment is turned against Endicott for his energetic initiative in destroying the May-Pole of Merry Mount, since it offered a choice between grim gloom and merry sunshine, and there is no indication that gloom was the better choice.

The attitude of the passenger of the Celestial Rail-road is unequivocal. As a parody of *Pilgrim's Progress*, it expresses a preference for the sterner Christianity of Bunyan over the easy-going liberalized religion of Mr. Smooth-it-away and his railroad. Indeed on his departure this guide is revealed to be a devil.

The narrator of *The Marble Faun*, like Hilda and Kenyon, is an American Protestant. His interest, like that of these characters, in the great religious art of Italy, is aesthetic rather than religious, as evidenced from the book being published as an illustrated guide to Rome. Italy is described as priest-ridden, its clergy ignorant, and superstitious. Notwithstanding this negative judgment, the book also presents Catholicism in a favorable light, especially its devotion to the Virgin Mother and the benefit of priestly confession.

Such in its main features is the attitude toward religion of our various narrators. Hawthorne the writer, of course, is the creator of these narrators as well as of the tales they told. Is Hawthorne the writer then to be identified with these narrators? And Hawthorne the man? To do so would be to make a very large assumption. There is very little evidence that Hawthorne the man was religious, certainly not as a regular, Church-going Christian. Hawthorne the writer was obviously interested in religion, since he wrote about it. But was that interest basically religious or aesthetic? Hawthorne is known to have been an avid reader and admirer of Bunyan's *Pilgrim's Progress*. But what was the basis and principal reason for that interest? Was it the religious teaching that it contained in offering a way of belief, worship, and practice? That is certainly doubtful. Nor is there any indication in the "Celestial Rail-road" that the passenger who narrates the story, despite his preference for the work of Bunyan, would actually follow the way of the Christian Pilgrim. The narrators and their narratives are the work of the imagination and art of Hawthorne the writer, and to suppose that they are identical with belief of Hawthorne the man is to lessen the creativity of the imagination and to deny the suspension of belief.

Endnotes

1   "Main Street" in *Tales and Sketches* (The Library of America, 1982), pp. 1030–31.

2   "Alice Doane's Appeal," *Tales*, p. 216.

3   "The Gentle Boy" in *Tales*, p. 108.

4   *Ibid.*, p. 128.

5   *Ibid.*, p. 138.

6   "Endicott and the Red Cross" in *Tales*, pp. 547–48.

7   *The Marble Faun* in *Novels* (The Library of America, 1983), p. 1074.

8   *Ibid.*, p. 1156.

9   *Ibid.*, p. 896.

10   *Ibid.*, pp. 941–42.

11   *Ibid.*, p. 1139.

12   *Ibid.*, p. 1138.

13   "Mrs. Hutchinson" in *Tales*, p. 19.

14   *Ibid.*, p. 23.

15   *Ibid.*, p. 21.

16   *Ibid.*, p. 24.

17   "The May-Pole of Merry Mount" in *Tales*, p. 368.

18   *Ibid.*, p. 366

19   "Hall of Fantasy" in *Tales*, p. 740.

20   *Ibid.*, pp. 740–41.

21   *Ibid.*, pp. 741–42.

22   *Ibid.*, p. 741.

23   "The Celestial Rail-road" in *Tales*, p. 811.

24   *Ibid.*, p. 817.

25   *Ibid.*, p. 818.

26   *Ibid.*, p. 824.

27   *The Blithedale Romance* in *Novels*, pp. 677–78.

28   *Ibid.*, p. 822.

29   *Ibid.*, p. 844

30   "Endicott and the Reed Cross," p. 548.

On Sin and Consequences

Introduction

"What is Guilt, "Hawthorne asked at the beginning of an early story entitled "Fancy's Show Box" (1837). Identifying sin as "a stain upon the soul," he then proceeded to inquire "Whether the soul may contract such stains, in all their depth and flagrancy, from deeds which may have been plotted and resolved upon, but which, physically, have never had existence."[1]

The story is subtitled "A Morality." Hawthorne the writer also elsewhere described his activity as burrowing "into the depths of our common nature for the purpose of psychological romance."[2]

These statements serve to indicate subjects and themes that are predominant in many of Hawthorne's writings: crimes and sins that men and women commit and their consequences, both good and evil, for their perpetrators as well as for those they affect.

The tales as well as the novels tell of many sins. They do so usually by recounting the actions and feelings of their malefactors rather than by an abstract analysis of their sins as such. Yet the results constitute an inquiry into the nature and effects of sin. And this subject, needless to say, is one that has been of great importance in religion, and not only to the Puritan forbears of Hawthorne.

The inquiry of "Fancy's Show Box" is carried out by venerable old Mr. Smith seated alone in his room with a glass of old

Madeira to whom Fancy presents pictures of scenes from his past life in which he might have sinned, which Memory judges and Conscience twinges. Three "ghosts of never perpetrated sins" appear.

The first presents the picture of a young man showing triumphant scorn over a kneeling girl prostrate at his feet – "the very image of his first love." Mr. Smith scandalized, bursts out, "Oh, vile and slanderous picture. . . . When have I triumphed over ruined innocence?" Memory, however, nudges him, and he recalls a situation that could apply to the picture, "a record merely of sinful thought, which never was embodied in an act." Conscience then "unveils her face, and strikes a dagger to the heart of Mr. Smith."[3]

The second is a scene of mirth and revelry among boon companions until it ends with a young man lying dead upon the floor – the earliest and best friend of Mr. Smith. The latter, "provoked beyond all patience," angrily denies that there had ever been such a murder. Memory, however, recalls an occasion on which both had been heated with wine, and had quarreled violently. Smith in great wrath had thrown a bottle at his friend, which fortunately missed him. But Conscience spoke again and "quelled his remonstrance."[4]

In the third scene Mr. Smith appears in the decline of life engaged in "stripping the clothes from the backs of three half-starved children." Smith filled with rectitude denounces it as a scandalous charge of robbing little children. Memory, however, recalls that he had been tempted to seize upon a legal quibble to question at law three orphans possessed of a large estate, and Conscience would have struck again had not her victim protected himself.

Faced thus with pictures of sins that Smith might have committed but did not, although his memory of them is fresh enough to arouse his conscience against him, what judgment can be brought against him? "Could such beings of cloudy fantasy, so near akin to nothingness, give valid evidence against him, at the day of judgment?" Conscience accuses him. Yet an argument can be made for his cause. It rests on the likeness there is between a scheme for a sin never committed and the plot of a projected tale. The tale "in order to produce a sense of reality in the reader's mind, must be conceived with such proportionate strength by the author as to seem, in the glow of fancy, more like truth, past, present, or to come, than purely fiction." So too, the prospective sinner plots his course of action, "but seldom or never feels a perfect certainty that it will be executed." Thus the novelist and the prospective sinner "may almost meet each other, half-way between reality and fancy."

But in regard to the question of guilt, "it is not until the crime is accomplished that guilt clenches its grip upon the guilty heart and claims it for its own. Then, and not before, sin is actually felt and acknowledged.[5] Hence the answer to the question posed at the beginning of the story is "that all the dreadful consequences of sin will not be incurred, unless the act have set its seal upon the thought."[6]

With this it would seem to be concluded that no guilt is incurred by the mere project of a possible sin without its actual execution. The lust, murder, and theft that Mr. Smith thought about but had not executed should then be no cause for feelings of guilt. The story might thus be read as comment upon the words of Jesus in the Gospel: "Ye have heard that it was said by them of old time, `Thou shalt not commit adultery.' But I say unto you. That whosoever looketh on a woman to lust after her hath committed adultery with her already in his heart." (Matt. 5:27–28)

Yet the conclusion reached in the story is not as unambiguous as indicated. For Mr. Smith still felt the pangs of conscience and what are these but an indication of guilt. We are told that "one truly penitential tear would have washed away each hateful picture, and left the canvass white as snow." Which is to say that a stain did exist. "But Mr. Smith, at a prick of Conscience too keen to be endured, bellowed aloud, with impatient agony. . . . His heart still seemed to fester with the venom of the dagger."[7] And the concluding paragraph declares: "Man must not disclaim his brotherhood, even the guiltiest, since, though his hand be clean, his heart has surely been polluted by the flitting phantoms of iniquity."[8]

Several of Hawthorne's tales consider a number of sins with the aim of locating and identifying one root sin that underlies all the others. A good example of this type is that one entitled "Egotism; or, the Bosom-Serpent." It tells the story of the hideous and agonizing transformation of the talented young Roderick. This change began, or first showed itself, when he separated from his wife. Gloom spread over his daily life; he estranged himself from all companionship. Then he engaged the service of noted quacks, one of whom administered a powder that rendered the patient insensible and, it is asserted, claimed that a snake had left his body. But Roderick still feels that a snake is gnawing at his bosom. He, acutely conscious of self, takes to seeking out the public, desirous not only of displaying it, but also of detecting the snake and declaring his find in a variety of persons: in a man who for thirty years had hated his own brother; a statesman whose ambition is identified as a boa constrictor; a close-fisted man of wealth who is said to have a copperhead; a drunk; a distinguished clergyman wrathful in controversy; a brooding, sickly sensitive person; a contentious married couple; an envious author constantly depreciating the books of others; a man of impure life; a young girl of shameful love; two women spitefully attacking one another; a jealous man. Roderick confronts each of these persons, names their particular sin, and ascribes its cause to the presence in each of them of a serpent.

In so doing, Roderick is said to be "making his own actual serpent – if a serpent there actually was in his bosom – the type of each man's fatal error, or hoarded sin, or unquiet conscience."

It is his theory that "every mortal bosom harbored either a brood of small serpents, or one overgrown monster, that had devoured all the rest."

Roderick is confined to an asylum for the insane, where his melancholy increases along with rage and hatred for his serpent and himself, and he attempts suicide unsuccessfully. Released from the asylum, he is visited by an old friend, a sculptor. In conversation with his friend, he loses all control of himself. Asked whether there is not a remedy for his plight, Roderick acknowledges that there is "but an impossible one. . . . Could I, for one instant, forget myself, the serpent might not abide within me. It is my diseased self-contemplation that has engendered and nourished him."[9]

The sculptor comments in conclusion: "Roger Elliston, whether the serpent was a physical reptile, or whether the morbidness of your nature suggested that symbol to your fantasy, the moral of the story is not the less true and strong. A tremendous Egotism – manifesting itself, in your case, in the form of jealousy – is as fearful a fiend as ever stole into the human heart."[10]

In the course of his walks about the city Roderick encounters a variety of sinners. In fact, he meets representatives or carriers of all the traditional seven capital or deadly sins and in each of them detects a different serpent: avarice in the person of the wealthy old man; gluttony in the brooding overly sensitive person; envy in the author; lust in the young girl of shame. The one element common to all of them is the presence of an indwelling snake.

What then is the snake? What does it typify? Roderick identifies it with his constant thought of self; his inability to think of anyone other than himself, his inability to forget himself, which his friend the sculptor, pointing the moral calls "a tremendous Egotism." Is snake in general then meant to stand for egotism, and the various kinds of snakes that are cited in the different sinners but so many ways in which egotism manifest itself?

Egotism, as Roderick sees it, is an excessive concern with self, an excessive love of self and hence an expression of pride. And pride is the worst of all the capital sins and the root of all the others. The people that Roderick meets can thus be regarded as so many different manifestations of pride.

Such excessive concern with self also reveals a lack of concern and love for another. Hence Roderick cannot free himself from his serpent until he "forget himself in the idea of another," as he does finally by being reunited with his wife.[11]

An even longer array of misery is presented in the story "The Christmas Banquet"; no less than thirty types of "the woefullest." It tells of an annual banquet for commemorating the ten most miserable people of the year. Four banquets are described as a celebration of misery, each person in attendance proud and boastful of his or her misery. All are interesting in a sad and sometimes comical way: the misanthrope who had become so from trusting others too much; the gallant man whose folly had turned sour; the beautiful solitary who had retired because of a cast in her left eye; the constitutionally merry gentleman under the threat of death from "cachinnatory indulgence" and who does die laughing; the rich stock broker who does not know that he is miserable; Father Miller in despair at the failure of the world's final conflagration he had foretold; the politician unable to find his party; the popular orator who has lost his voice. But through all the annual banquets there is one person who attends every year from his youth until his old age. He is often criticized by others as not qualifying for the group from his obvious lack of misery. Yet he is constantly invited by the overseers of the banquet. He is booed for being "cold, cold." And at the end of his life he declares that he is "the sole unfortunate of the human race." He declares, "Mine is the wretchedness! This cold heart – this unreal life! Ah! it grows colder still." Among all these "moral monsters," it is the person of cold heart who is the worst of all, the one who seems "to be outside of everything."[12]

Several other stories emphasize the same moral by identifying the worst depravity with coldness of heart. "Ethan Brand" recounts the story of the man bearing that name who spends his life seeking for the "Unpardonable Sin," some mode of guilt which could neither be atoned for nor forgiven."[13] According to the Gospel, the Lord declared: "Verily I say unto you, All sins shall be forgiven unto the son of men, and blasphemies wherewithsoever they shall blaspheme: But he that shall blaspheme against the Holy Ghost hast never forgiveness, but is in danger of eternal damnation." (Mk 3:28–29)

Interpreters of the Bible disagree about the identification of this unpardonable sin. Yet Ethan Brand is convinced that he has found it: "Standing erect with the pride that distinguishes all enthusiasts of his stamp," he declares that it is "the sin of an intellect that triumphed over the sense of brotherhood with man and reverence for God, and sacrificed everything to its own mighty claims!"[14] In the beginning Ethan Brand had been a simple limeburner filled with tenderness, love, and sympathy for mankind, had looked reverently into the heart of men and had pitied their woe.

> Then ensued that vast intellectual development, which, in its progress, disturbed the counterpoise between his mind and heart . . . it had raised him from an unlettered laborer, to stand on a star-lit eminence. . . . But where was the heart? That, indeed, had withered – had contracted – had hardened – had perished . . . he was now a cold observer, looking on mankind as the subject of his experiment. . . . Thus Ethan Brand became a fiend.[15]

Brand, like Hastings in the "The Christmas Banquet," is revealed in the end to be cold at heart, frozen in his pride. Dante too when he reached the depths of hell, where pride typifies the worst and greatest of all sins, finds that its greatest malefactors are frozen in ice. So too "The Man of Adamant" portrays the pride of an ancient Puritan as petrified within the cave of his dwelling into a statue "in the attitude of repelling the whole race of mortals – not from Heaven – but from the horrible loneliness of his dark, cold sepulchre."[16]

Is sin or the tendency to commit it congenital with the nature of human beings? And besides being with them from birth is it also something that can be inherited from generation to generation? Hawthorne seems to give affirmative answers to both questions in the tales, and they become of major importance in the great novels.

"Earth's Holocaust" tells of a reform movement that aimed to rid the world of its "accumulation of worn-out trumpery . . . by a general bonfire" so as to make it possible to start afresh without the injustice and misery that it caused. We witness many of the things that had long been treasured thrown onto a huge fire. But while it is still in progress a skeptical observer expresses doubt that it can ever achieve its intended purpose: "There is one thing that these wiseacres have forgotten to throw into the fire, and without which all the rest of the conflagration is just nothing at all – yes, though they had burnt the earth itself to a cinder." Asked what might be, the stranger replies: "What, but the human heart itself! . . . And unless they hit upon some method of purifying that foul cavern, forth from it will re-issue all the shapes of wrong and misery – the same old shapes or worse ones.[17] This observation leads the narrator to conclude that "Man's age-long endeavor for perfection had served only to render him the mockery of the Evil Principle, from the fatal circumstance of an error at the very root of the matter! The Heart – the Heart – there was the little, yet boundless sphere, wherein existed the original wrong, of which the crime and mystery of this outward world were merely types."[18]

Young Goodman Brown, in the story of that name, attends in a dream a witch-meeting in the forest. There he finds that many men and women, both young and old, reputed to be virtuous and with a good reputation, are there to wait upon the Devil himself, who addressing them declares:

By the sympathy of your human hearts for sin, ye shall
scent out all the places – whether in church, bed-chamber,
street, field, or forest – where crime has been committed,
and shall exult to behold on the whole earth one stain of
guilt, one mighty blood-spot. . . . Depending upon one
another's hearts, ye had still hoped that virtue were not all
a dream. Now are ye undeceived! Evil is the nature of
mankind. Evil must be your only happiness."[19]

The Scarlet Letter

Hawthorne's first novel, or Romance, as he called it, deals at
length and in detail with the consequences of sin and not with
the sin that was their cause. When the story opens the sin of
adultery already had been discovered by the birth of a daughter
to Hester Prynne, a married woman who for two years had been
living alone in Boston while her husband remained in Europe.
The Puritan community had already judged Hester's adultery a
sin and her exposure in the pillory and the wearing of a scarlet
A "upon her dress as a badge and avowal of her sinful deed. The
daughter, Pearl, was the first expressed consequence of that sin,
but Hester takes pride in her, as the girl's name indicated, recall-
ing the Gospel parable of the 'pearl of great price.'" (Matt. 13:46)
The punishment of wearing, even displaying, the scarlet letter,
incites and motivates the ensuing actions that affect not only
Hester, but also the other principal characters, Arthur
Dimmesdale, the Puritan minister and until the end, the unac-
knowledged lover of Hester and father of her child, and Roger
Chillingworth, Hester's legal husband who appears in Boston
just as she is beginning her punishment.

The sin's effect upon Dimmesdale also first occurred in public at the scaffold where Hester was pilloried, surrounded by the
public at large, and also by the officials of state and church who
had condemned her. The governor appealed directly to
Dimmesdale as Hester's spiritual adviser to persuade her to

repent and confess, declaring "the responsibility of this woman's soul lies greatly with you." The reader who knows the outcome of the story can appreciate the irony of the governor's remark, since Dimmesdale bears a far heavier responsibility than was literally intended. Ironic, too, is Dimmesdale's own appeal to Hester to reveal the name of the child's father saying:

> Be not silent from any mistaken pity and tenderness for him: for believe me, Hester, though he were to step down from a high place, and stand there before thee, on thy Pedestal of shame, yet better were it so, than to hide a guilty heart through life. What can Thy silence do for him, except to tempt him – yea, compel him, as it were – to add hypocrisy to sin? Heaven hath granted thee an open ignominy, that thereby thou mayest work out an open triumph over the evil within thee, and the sorrow without. Take heed how thou deniest to him – who, perchance, hath not the courage to grasp it for himself.[20]

However, despite appeals and commands and even the knowledge that she would be able to remove the scarlet letter, Hester refused to name her lover, upon which Dimmesdale exclaimed, "Wondrous strength and generosity of a woman's heart!"[21]

One might also add love to strength and generosity, as Hester's subsequent actions bore out. But from what Dimmesdale said about the father who is unknown to the crowd, Hester and the reader know that the words apply to him. With them, Dimmesdale began to suffer the consequences of his sin: a guilty heart and the hypocrisy of one who lacks the courage to admit his wrong.

The sin's effect upon Chillingworth began when he recognized that the woman on the scaffold was Hester, his wife. "A writhing horror twisted itself across his features, like a snake gliding swiftly over them";[22] the reader may recall the bosom-snake of the story of that name. Told that his wife will not reveal the name of the father, Chillingworth declared, "He will be known! He will be known! He will be known! And thereby already takes up that task."[23] The seed of revenge has been planted.

The sin for which Hester wore the scarlet letter has begun to give birth to further sins. The ensuing actions reveal how sin worked itself out in the lives of the persons it had infected. Hester, in bearing her punishment and working to support herself and her daughter, grew in strength of character. Dimmesdale, in concealing and refusing to acknowledge his sin, increased his hypocrisy as well as his suffering both in conscience and body until he can find release through public confession. Chillingworth, in claiming to treat Dimmesdale medically, added to the latter's torment and himself plunged deeper into evil.

Hester at first appeared to get more deeply mired in trouble. She had refused to identify her lover. But when Chillingworth gained an interview with her and persuaded her not to reveal his identity under the new name he had assumed, Hester committed herself to keeping two secrets: the first at her own desire for the sake of her lover; the second at the request of her husband, which she grants perhaps out of fear and shame. She admitted that she had wronged him. But Chillingworth asserted that he also had wronged her, his folly being "the first wrong, when I betrayed thy budding youth into a false and unnatural relation with my decay."[24] But Chillingworth claimed that he had also been wronged by Hester's lover, and said that he can – and will – discover his name. "No matter whether of love or hate; no matter whether of right or wrong! Thou and thine, Hester Prynne, belong to me," Chillingworth declared. Hester swears to keep secret his identity and not reveal it especially to her lover, for "Should thou fail me in this, beware! His fame, his position, his life, will be in my hands."[25] Troubled at the expression in Chillingworth's eyes, Hester asked, "Art thou like the

Black Man that haunts the forest round about us? Hast though enticed me into a bond that will prove the ruin of my soul?" And her husband answered, "Not thy soul. No, not thine."[26] Whose then? His own? Dimmesdale's"?

By remaining in Boston to bear her punishment, Hester chose to suffer the scornful and condemning eyes of all she met. She could flee to a place where she was not known and then would not have had to wear the letter of shame. Yet she did not.

> What she compelled herself to believe, – what finally she reasoned upon, as her motive for continuing a resident of New England, – was half a truth, and half a self-delusion. Here, she said to herself, had been the scene of her guilt, and here should be the scene of her earthly punishment; and so, perchance, the torture of her daily shame would at length purge her soul, and work out another purity than that which she had lost; more saint-like, because the result of martyrdom.[27]

Was she deceiving herself? If so, how? Certainly not through any hope that she would escape torment. The people she lived among would see to that. Then is it because she hoped to achieve a more saint-like purity?

A foreboding sense of possible sin tortured Hester's conscience. First, because she feared that her union with her lover might "bring them together before the bar of final judgment, and make that their marriage altar, for a joint futurity of endless retribution."[28] Next, Hester rejected as sin her skill at exquisite needlework,[29] perhaps because of her pride in it. Greatly appreciated for her gifted needlework, Hester supported both herself and little Pearl through it. Finally, even when Hester encountered what she takes as a look of commiseration in the eyes of another, she at once felt that "she had sinned anew." In fact, she felt or fancied then that "the scarlet letter had endowed her with a new sense . . . a sympathetic knowledge of the hidden sin other hearts." This sense horrified her since "Hester Prynne yet struggled to believe that no fellow-mortal was guilty like herself."[30] Even her love for her daughter was tainted by her sense of sin. "She knew that her deed had been evil; she could have no faith, therefore, that its result would be for good."[31] Yet she never ceased to care for Pearl, watch over her, teach her the Catechism, and dress her splendidly.

The relationship between Chillingworth and Dimmesdale gradually became more entwined, at least socially, than either one had with Hester. Chillingworth soon established himself as the chief doctor of medicine in the town where none of note existed previously. He showed himself exemplary in his religious duties, at least in observance of their outward forms. He took particular interest in the Puritan divine, becomes a parishioner of his church, and watched with apparent concern the deteriorating health of the young clergyman. This condition aroused the concern of the church elders and the leading parishioners so greatly that they prevailed upon the clergyman to consult the doctor about his health. As a result of Dimmesdale's worsening health in both body and mind and the interest and wiles of Doctor Chillingworth, the two soon were living together under the same roof. This made it possible for the doctor to keep his patient under almost constant observation and in frequent conversations.

Since his arrival in town and especially after taking resident with Dimmesdale, Chillingworth had undergone a remarkable change in his appearance:

> At first his expression had been calm, meditative, scholarlike. Now there was something ugly and evil in his face" which others "had not previously noted, and which grew still the more obvious to sight, the oftener they looked upon him.[32]

In fact, it came to be thought that the clergyman, "like many other personages of sanctity, in all ages of the Christian world, was haunted either by Satan himself, or Satan's emissary, in the guise of old Roger Chillingworth."[33]

The doctor took a fierce even fanatical interest in his patient, prying in every way he could to penetrate into the soul as well as the body of the poor minister. Dimmesdale became "vaguely aware that something inimical to his peace had thrust itself into relation with him."[34] One day the two chanced to talk about the wisdom of divulging a secret. The doctor asserted a guilty one is bound to come out. But this the clergyman denied, claiming that "the heart, making itself guilty of such secrets, must per-force hold them, until the day when all hidden things shall be revealed." He then provided in effect a defense of his own con-duct, or at least a reason for it: Such men

> guilty as they may be, retaining, nevertheless, a zeal for God's glory and man's welfare, they shrink from displaying themselves black and filthy in the view of men; because, henceforward, no good can be achieved by them; no evil of the past be redeemed by better service.[35]

At this point the reason that Dimmesdale gave for accepting his torment is much like that of Hester; both undergo it for the sake of achieving a further good.

After seeing Hester and Pearl go past their window, conver-sation resumed. Chillingworth continued talking about the sub-ject of guilty secrets and asked whether in Hester's case, when her sin was known, she was less miserable for the scarlet letter that she wore. "I do verily believe it," Dimmesdale answered, asserting that "it must needs be better for the sufferer to be free to show his pain as this poor woman, Hester, is than to cover it all up in his heart."[36] Following up this line attack, the doctor inquired whether he might not be able to help his patient more if "all the operation of this disorder [has] been fairly laid open and recounted." Dimmesdale refused to reveal more, noting that if his was a disease of the soul it must be committed to "the one Physician of the soul."[37]

But, although Dimmesdale revealed no more by speech, Chillingworth learned immensely more. For soon afterwards he came upon the clergyman at noontime in a deep sleep. He thrust aside the vestment that always covered Dimmesdale's chest. The physician turned away, "but with what a wild look of wonder, joy, and horror! . . . Had a man seen old Roger Chillingworth, at that moment of ecstasy, he would have had no need to ask how Satan comports himself, when a precious human soul is lost to heaven, and won into his kingdom". Yet there was something more: "What distinguished the physician's ecstasy from Satan's was the trait of wonder in it."[38] Thus Chillingworth had pierced the clergyman's guilty secret that had itself pierced the man's flesh. Chillingworth had discovered, as he boasted he would, the identity of the man who had wronged him as a husband, and he might now be expected to work his revenge to any extent that he desired.

But although Chillingworth achieved his revenge, it was not all that he may have desired and certainly was not entirely of his doing. Dimmesdale and Hester became increasingly the agents of their destiny. As a result of his discovery, Chillingworth's malice increased and he hoped to force the priest to confess to him the guilty secret, the remorseful agony: "All that dark treasure to be lavished on the very man, to whom nothing else could so adequately pay the debt of vengeance!"[39] But in this he failed even as he became a "chief actor in the poor minister's interior world." Dimmesdale's torment increased not only because of his tormentor, but also because of the great popularity that he achieved as a preacher. He possessed what others lacked, "the gift that descended upon the chosen disciples, at Pentecost, in tongues of flames; symbolizing, it would seem, not the power of speech in foreign and unknown languages, but that of addressing the whole human brotherhood in the heart's native language." The inward burden that he bore "gave him sympathies so intimate with the sinful brotherhood of mankind; so that his heart vibrated in union with theirs."[40] Yet this talent with its accompanying success only added to the anguish of the minister by deepening the sense of his hypocrisy. It drove him "to practices, more in accordance with the old, corrupted faith of

Rome, than with the better light of the church in which he had been born and bred."[41] He took to scourging himself, he kept nightly vigils and fasts, all of which "typified the constant intro-spect wherewith he tortured, but could not purify, himself."[42]

One such midnight vigil drove Dimmesdale to the first external expression of his guilt. Driven by remorse and cow-ardice and in the dark while the town was asleep, the minister mounted the scaffold on which Hester had first been compelled to expose her sin and shame. There without willing it or power to repress it, "he shrieked aloud," and feared immediately that the whole town might waken to witness his exposure. That did not occur; however, the three persons closest to him discovered him there. Seeing Hester and Pearl returning from attending the governor on his deathbed, the minister invited them to join him on the scaffold. There, hand in hand, the three stood, and the minister felt "what seemed a tumultuous rush of new life, other life than his own."[43] Chillingworth also appeared, surprising Dimmesdale especially so that he appealed in terror to Hester: "Who is that man. . . . I shiver at him! Dost thou know the man? I hate him."[44] But Hester remembered her oath and said noth-ing. The minister returned home with his tormentor.

The midnight vigil led Hester to reconsider her own respon-sibilities. She was greatly shocked by the condition to which Dimmesdale had been reduced, and she suspected that Chillingworth had contributed much to bring that about. Hester herself had matured and changed much during the seven years that she had been wearing the scarlet letter. She had not only led a pure and virtuous life, but had also become "a self-ordained Sister of Mercy." She had proven so much a source of strength to those in need that many people refused to interpret the scarlet A by its original signification. They said it meant "Able."[45] She saw after the vigil that the man she loved needed her strength.

Hester, in considering the minister's racked condition, asked herself whether she must not bear some of the blame for it: "whether there had originally been a defect of truth, courage and loyalty, on her own part, in allowing the minister to be thrown into a position where so much evil was to be foreboded, and nothing suspicious to be hoped."[46] This she had done by promising not to reveal the identity of her husband, believing that this would prevent Dimmesdale from experiencing a still worse ruin. "Under that impulse, she had made her choice, and had chosen, as it now appeared, the more wretched alternative of the two."[47] She determined to confront Chillingworth and take back her oath.

In the interview Hester sought out with the physician, she was much struck, as she had been by that of the minister, by the bodily changes the old man had undergone. No longer calm and quiet, he had "an angry, searching, almost fierce, yet carefully guarded look. . . . Even and anon, too, there came a glare of red light out of his eyes; as if the old man's soul were on fire. . . . In a word, old Roger Chillingworth was a striking evidence of man's faculty of transforming himself into a devil, if he will only, for a reasonable space of time, undertake a devil's office."[48]

Hester accused the physician of cruelly and evilly torment-ing the minister, who had imagined that he was being tortured by the devil, whereas in fact "there was a fiend at his elbow! A mortal man, with once a human heart, has become a fiend for his especial torment!"[49] At this accusation, a look of horror appeared on the physician's face – "one of those moments . . . when a man's moral aspect is faithfully revealed to his mind's eye."[50] But the moment passed instantly, although it permitted the whole evil within him to be written on his features. Admitting he had become a fiend, Chillingworth asked who made him so, and Hester confessed that it was indeed she. But, she added, if so, he should have avenged himself on her, not on the minister. Whatever may come of it, Hester said, she intend-ed to reveal the secret so that Dimmesdale may know the true character of his physician. Thereby she will have paid "this long debt of confidence, due from me to him, whose bane and ruin I have been."[51] Hester called upon Chillingworth to forget and forgive, to purge out "the hatred that has transformed a wise and just man to a fiend."[52] But he replied: "it is not granted me to pardon," and the evil must work itself out.

Yet Hester cannot deny that she hated the old man whom she now realized it had been a mistake to marry, maintaining that "he has done me worse wrong that I did him." The violence of her passion at the confrontation raised the question: "Had seven long years, under the torture of the scarlet letter, inflicted so much of misery, and wrought out no repentance?"[53] Then when queried by her daughter about the meaning of the scarlet letter, Hester lied, saying "for the sake of its gold thread." For the first time she was false to that symbol. What moved her to do so? "It may be that it was the talisman of a stern and severe, but yet a guardian spirit, who now forsook her; as recognizing that, in spite of his strict watch her heart, some new evil had crept into it, or some old one had never been expelled."[54] Thus although Hester may heroically bear her shameful punishment, she has not been purged of all sin.

Later Hester met the minister in the forest as he was returning to his home from a visit. He bared his anguish to her, the torment that he suffered over his consciousness of sin and the reverence his parishioners had for his holy life. As he said, "I have laughed, in bitterness and agony of heart, at the contrast between what I seem and what I am! And Satan laughs at it!"[55] Hester tried to comfort him, unsuccessfully. Then, aware that Chillingworth's malignity must have sorely added to the minister's suffering, she confessed, revealing that he was her husband. She acknowledged her fault in keeping that secret for such a time, expressed sorrow for the pain it had brought, and pled for forgiveness.

This is the only time that readers witness Hester and Arthur Dimmesdale giving expression to their love for one another. For a while they even fondly dream of fleeing and escaping from the horror under which each was suffering. Dimmesdale declared: "I freely forgive you now. May God forgive us both! We are not,

Hester, the worst sinners in the world. There is one worse than even the polluted priest! That old man's revenge has been blacker than my sin." And Hester commented, "What we did has a consecration of its own."[56]

The minister on returning alone to his house felt himself in a maze and a changed man. Yet at first he doubted whether was for the better. For on his way he encountered a series of temptations to mock and flout his religious and moral principles, which he was able to restrain only with difficulty. At home he again met Chillingworth, and although not expressly confronting and accusing him, Dimmesdale believed that they both knew they are the bitterest enemies.

The Election Day on which the new governor took office witnessed both Arthur Dimmesdale's greatest triumph as a preacher and his public confession and fall. Hester and Pearl hear the sermon as they stand just outside the meetinghouse by the scaffold where the scarlet letter had been first publicly displayed. In the sound of the preacher's voice Hester detected expressions of anguish, cries of pain, that left the auditors at the end of the sermon filled with awe and wonder. Then, in a state of near collapse, Dimmesdale left the church and joined Hester and Pearl at the scaffold. Chillingworth, guessing what the minister was about to do, caught him by the arm and sought to dissuade him from joining the woman and her child, but Dimmesdale threw him off and asked Hester to help support him onto the scaffold. There together with mother and child he addressed the tumultuous crowd, declaring:

> At last! – at last! – I stand upon the spot where, seven years
> since, I should have stood. . . . Lo, the scarlet letter which
> Hester wears! Ye have all shuddered at it! Wherever the
> walk hath been – wherever, so miserably cast a lurid gleam
> of awe and horrible repugnance round about her. But there
> stood one in the midst of you, at whole brand of sin and
> infamy ye have not shuddered! . . . Now, at the death-hour,
> he stands up before you! He bids you look again at Hester's

mysterious horror, it is but the shadow of what he bears on his own breast, and that even this, his own red stigma, is no more than the type of what has seared his inmost heart![57]

Dimmesdale then tore away his clothing to expose for all to see the scarlet letter in the flesh of his chest, and collapsed upon the scaffold. Hester raised him so as to support his head upon her bosom. Old Chillingworth knelt beside them, declaring more than once, "Thou has escaped me," as the minister called upon God to forgive him. Hester whispered to the dying man her hope that might spend their immortal life together. To which Dimmesdale responded, "Hush, Hester, Hush! . . . The law we broke – the sin here so awfully revealed! Let these alone be in thy thoughts. . . . God knows, and He is merciful! He hath proved his mercy most of all in my afflictions." And saying, "Praised be his name! His will be done! Farewell![58] Arthur Dimmesdale died.

The events occurring over a period of seven years, as narrated, witness the transformation physically as well as spiritually, of three human beings. Of the three Hester emerged as the strongest. She daily bore the stigma of her shame and yet became the nobler for it. Yet she cannot but show the results of her suffering:

> All the light and graceful foliage of her character had been withered up by this red-hot brand, and had long ago fallen away, leaving a bare and harsh outline. . . . Even the attractiveness of her person had undergone a similar change. . . . It was a sad transformation, too, that her rich and luxuriant hair had either been cut off, or was so completely hidden by a cap, that not shining lock of it ever once gushed into the sunshine. . . . Some attribute had departed from her, the permanence of which had been essential to keep her a woman.[59]

Nor had her suffering entirely purged Hester of evil and sin. She had concealed from her lover her relationship to Chillingworth and thus had contributed to the suffering that the latter was able to inflict. Nor could she overcome her hatred for the old man who was her husband. Yet at the end she stood up to Chillingworth and supported the minister as she made known the relation among the three, and thereby helped her lover to overcome his cowardice and hypocrisy by publicly confessing his sin.

Of the three, Dimmesdale is the weakest. He also suffered the greatest anguish from the sin that he cannot rid himself of, and physically showed the most physical deterioration, so much so that it ultimately led to collapse and death. His sins were compounded from the initial act of adultery, then the failure to admit it, thereby allowing Hester to bear the punishment alone, the hypocrisy of the life he led as a preacher known for holiness and his developing hatred for the tormentor with whom he lives. Yet through his suffering Dimmesdale came to overcome these failings. He forgave Hester for what she had done in concealing the identity of Chillingworth, whom he also forgave, and in the last of his life joined Hester and Pearl upon the scaffold of pillory and confessed to the public his own most grievous fault.

Chillingworth is much the worst of the three. His desire for vengeance and active pursuit of it plunged him ever more deeply into evil. For one brief moment under the accusation of Hester, he seemed to acknowledge his guilt, but he immediately cast aside that judgment and even bragged that he had become a fiend. He refused to forgive Dimmesdale and as the latter lies dying can think only that he is being cheated of the full revenge that he desired. There is no sign whatsoever of repentance on his part, except for the one admission that he had been at fault in marrying the beautiful young Hester when he was already a withered old man.

The only redeeming act Chillingworth performed was in willing his wealth to little Pearl upon his death, which occurred soon after that of his victim.

The unhappy man had made the very principle of his life to consist in the pursuit and systematic exercise of revenge; and when, by its completest triumph and consumation, that evil principle was left with no further material to support it, – when, in short, there was no more devil's work on earth for him to do, it only remained for the unhumanized mortal to betake himself whether his Master would find him tasks enough and pay him his wages duly.[60]

The House of the Seven Gables

The second long work by Hawthorne like the *Scarlet Letter* is also introduced as a "romance." This form as distinguished from the novel is defended as one that allows for greater freedom in its construction so as to emphasize with imaginative detail the truth that it seeks to portray. It can even unabashedly propose a thesis that the tale can portray and thus demonstrate. The Preface calls it a "moral" and states it as "the truth, namely, that the wrong-doing of one generation lives into the successive one, and, divesting itself of every temporary advantage, becomes a pure and uncontrollable mischief."[61]

Hence this second romance continues to deal with sin and its consequences, but unlike the first these consequences extend over a much longer period of time, in fact, over generations and almost two hundred years. Although the time of the action is narrated as occurring in the present of the narrator, the story has to take into account the activities and sufferings of the leading persons in the previous generations, since these originate the sins and develop the consequences that ultimately lead to the disclosure of the evil.

The story concerns two families, the Pynchons and the Maules, and one building, the centuries-old oaken-timbered house of the seven gables. The ground on which the house was erected provided the occasion for the originating sin that infects and poisons the succeeding generations of the two families.

The trouble began with an act of covetousness by old Colonel Pynchon, a strong, energetic, unscrupulous soldier and magistrate of a 17th-century Puritan colony in the County of Essex, Mass. In the pride of his success the colonel desired to display his wealth by building a mansion. But it happened that the plot of ground on which he wanted to build was owned by Matthew Maule, an obscure man compared to the colonel, but equally stubborn in holding to what he considered his right. The colonel claimed the land was his by a grant of legislature, although there was suspicion that the claim may have been "unduly stretched." The controversy gave no sign of being resolved and was not until death intervened. Old Maule was accused of witchcraft, an accusation strongly supported by Col. Pynchon, and executed. The personal enmity between the two men was widely known, and at the moment of execution Maule uttered a curse against the Colonel watching the hanging: "God will give him blood to drink."[62]

Col. Pynchon then obtained the land he desired and proceeded to erect his mansion over the very spot where Maule had had his log cabin, thereby building his house, it was said, over an unquiet grave. Ironically, the chief carpenter and architect of the Pynchon house of the seven gables was Thomas Maule, son of the executed wizard. The house completed, plans were made for having a great house-warming. But on the very day of the festivity and after the many guests had arrived, the colonel failed to appear. He was then found in his study, with blood on his ruff and his beard saturated with it, seated at his desk before a map on the wall, presumably of lands in Maine that he lay claim to, and a large portrait of himself. Col. Pynchon died a wealthy man, but his wealth did not turn out to be as great as reputed. His heir was never able to find the title deed to the extensive lands in Maine that were supposed to be his. His descendants for years after persisted in asserting their right to these lands, but unsuccessfully since they lacked the proof. "This impalpable claim, therefore, resulted in nothing more solid than to cherish, from generation to generation, an absurd delusion of family importance."[63] Yet it also resulted time and again in further acts of covetousness.

The old colonel's sin had resulted in the charge of witchcraft being made against Matthew Maule. The second sin of covetousness by a Pynchon led to the injury and eventual death of a beloved Pynchon. This consequence came about in the life of the colonel's grandson, Gervayse. This Pynchon inherited wealth and lived extravagantly off it, spending most of his time in Europe. In straightened circumstances and greedy for more, he undertook a search for the missing deed to the Maine lands. For this purpose he sought out the help of Old Maule's grandson, Matthew who was also a carpenter. There was a tradition among both the Pynchon and Maule families, that something of this secret was known by the Maules. Young Maule agreed to undertake the search for the missing deed, but only at a price. He wanted possession of the old Pynchon mansion of the seven gables and a talk with Gervayse's daughter Alice. The first condition was readily accepted, but the second was granted only with great reluctance. Alice — young, beautiful, and haughty – was introduced to young Matthew Maule. But the latter was upset and angered by the contemptuous pride of the girl and acted at once to avenge it. He had inherited some of the wizardry that his grandfather possessed, and in the course of a short meeting he succeeded in gaining control of Alice's mind so that henceforth she had to give way to the slightest thought that he directed her way. The result was close to lunacy on the part of the girl, and after many ludicrous, and unseemly actions, she took sick and died. Maule was furious at this outcome. "He meant to humble Alice, not to kill her; – but he had taken a woman's delicate soul into his rude gripe, to play with; – and she was dead."[64]

Maule repudiated the proposition that Gervayse Pynchon had offered and declared: "The custody of this secret, that would so enrich his heirs, makes part of your grandfather's retribution. He must choke with it, until it is no longer of any value. And keep you the House of the Seven Gables! It is too dear bought an inheritance, and too heavy, with the curse upon it, to be shifted yet awhile from the Colonel's posterity."[65]

Blame for this second sin thus did not lie entirely upon a Pynchon, as the first initiating one did. For old Col. Pynchon seems to have instigated the work entirely by himself, leaving Old Maule to blame only for his stubbornness, unless some evil act of his lay behind the accusation of witchcraft. However, the relation between Gervayse Pynchon and young Maule is a more complicated one. Pride and greed were clearly displayed by the Pynchon man as well as a betrayal of his daughter Alice. Yet the hatred of Maule for the Pynchons and his bitterness toward what he regarded as their treachery was no less evident, and still worse was his destruction of the mind and will of the beautiful Alice.

The next sin occurred during the life of the Pynchons whose actions, thoughts, and feelings are the principal concern of the narrative. Yet the sin and crime the consequences of which are worked out took place some thirty years before the main characters appear. The head of the Pynchons was then Uncle Jaffrey, a bachelor of great wealth who possessed the old mansion and all that remained of the Pynchon lands. Of a melancholic cast of mind with an interest in the records and traditions of the family, he became convinced that the original Maule had been wrongly deprived of his land and perhaps also of his life. So convinced, and as an unusual Pynchon with a conscience, he contemplated to make restitution to Maule posterity.

> To a man living so much in the past, and so little in the present, as the secluded and antiquarian old bachelor, a century and a half seemed not so vast a period as to obviate the propriety of substituting right for wrong.[66]

But the ideas of losing so much wealth so aroused the relatives that the conscientious old man never acted upon his conviction. Nor upon his death did his will change matters. His wealth passed down yet again unto Pynchons.

Of these there were no longer many. The chief inheritor was a nephew, named after his uncle Jaffrey, who later became prominent as a lawyer and judge, a niece Hepzibah from another side of the family and her brother Clifford, and a distant country-cousin named Phoebe. The house went to the niece on a life interest; the rest and bulk of the wealth went to the man who became a judge.

Yet from the start the inheritance was implicated in mystery and sin. The old bachelor uncle was found dead in curious circumstances, seeming to have choked in his own blood, dressed only in his night clothes in the study which had been ransacked. Murder was suspected, the nephew Clifford was accused, successfully prosecuted for it, and sent to prison where for thirty years he wasted away until his release.

The unfolding and disclosing of this latest of the sins of the Pynchons, itself following upon their many preceding ones, began when Clifford returns to the house of the seven gables to join his devoted sister Hepzibah.

"Hepzibah" is a Biblical name, and Isaiah's words in which it occurs apply to the Pynchon old maid: "Thou shalt no more be termed Forsaken; neither shalt they land any more be termed Desolate: but thou shalt be called Hepzibah, and they land Beulah: for the Lord delighteth in these, and thy land shall be married." – Isa. 62:4

For the past thirty years at the time Hepzibah Pynchon appears in the narrative she had felt forsaken and the decaying old mansion in which she had lived for all her sixty years had indeed been desolate. For her brother Clifford, to whom she was greatly and dearly devoted had been taken from her and imprisoned for a crime of which she felt that he was innocent. But now after those thirty years he had been released and was coming home.

Hepzibah was not without her faults. She was very proud of her Pynchon descent and considered herself a "born and educated lady . . . with her deeply cherished and ridiculous consciousness of long descent, her shadowy claims to princely territory."[67] Yet she was in fact a poor forlorn old maid who had been a recluse all her life. Despite her pride her appearance told against her. Her shortsightedness gave her a perpetual scowl which was interpreted by others as a sign of ill-temper. Although very poor, her hatred and distrust of her cousin the judge led her to refuse any offer of financial help from him. Yet with the return of Clifford to live with her, she had to increase her income. This she attempted by opening a penny shop in her house, however much it hurt her pride. Yet beneath and despite such shortcomings, she was naturally tender, sensitive, and willing to help others, so that it could be said of her:

> Truly was there something high, generous, and noble, in the native composition of our poor old Hepzibah! Or else . . . she had been enriched by poverty, developed by sorrow, elevated by the strong and solitary affection of her life, and thus endowed with heroism, which never could have characterized her in what are called happier circumstances. . . . In her own behalf, she had asked nothing of Providence, but the opportunity of devoting herself to this brother whom she had so loved – so admired for what he was, or might have been - - and to whom she had kept her faith, alone of all the world, wholly, unfalteringly, at every instant, and throughout life.[68]

Clifford Pynchon, the brother, after serving thirty years of his prison sentence returned to his home a broken man. He had always possessed a nature of exceptional sensitivity with something feminine in it and responsive to all forms of beauty. "It seemed Clifford's nature to be a Sybarite."[69] But prison had left him a fragmentary person: Continually "he faded away out of his place; or . . . his mind and consciousness took their departure, leaving him wasted, gray, and melancholy figure – a substantial emptiness, a material ghost."[70] He had been made for happiness, and, thwarted of that, his sensitivity had turned him into a worse person. His irritability was extreme and his selfishness such that he could not but give expression to it. The worst instance of this failing showed in his treatment of his sister:

> The hardest stroke of fate for Hepzibah to endure, and perhaps for Clifford too – was his invincible distaste for her appearance. Her features, never the most agreeable, and now harsh with age and grief, and resentment against the world for his sake; her dress, . . . the queer and quaint matters, which had unconsciously grown upon her in solitude; such being the poor gentlewoman's outward characteristics, it is no great marvel although the mournfullest of pities, that the instinctive lover of the Beautiful was fain to turn away his eyes.[71]

Hepzibah, who would have given her life and all she had to serve her brother, was aware of his distaste for her appearance. In her love for him she turned to the young and pretty Phoebe, the country cousin who had come to live with her. Phoebe is all innocence, prettiness, and practicality, and since Hepzibah can find no trace of the curse of the Pynchons in the girl declares that she must take after her mother and not her father. Although the old maid was at first doubtful of allowing her to stay at the seven gables, her pleasant manners and great helpfulness soon made Phoebe indispensable to both of her old cousins. Her "country-birth and residence in truth, had left her pitifully ignorant of most of the family traditions, which lingered like cobwebs and incrustation of smoke, about the rooms and chimney-corners of the House of the Seven Gables."[72] Yet when she first met the head of the family in the person of the august Judge Pynchon she was frightened of him and instinctively withdrew herself as he attempted to bestow a kiss upon the pretty cousin.

> "The truth was . . . that, although Judge Pynchon's glowing benignity might not be absolutely unpleasant to the feminine beholder, with the width of a street or even an ordi-

nary sized room interposed between, yet it became quite
too intense, when the dark full-fed physiognomy, (so
roughly bearded too, that no razor could ever make it
smooth) sought to bring itself into actual contact with the
object of its regards. The man, the sex, somehow or other,
was entirely too prominent in the Judge's demonstrations
of that sort." And Phoebe thought "He looks as if there
were nothing softer in him than a rock, nor milder than the
east wind."[73]

Phoebe by nature had not the slightest tinge of morbidity
about it, and under her busy and cheerful ministrations the very
gloom of the decaying old mansion seemed to be lifted as were
the drooping and pitiful spirits of both Hepzibah and Clifford.
"Whatever health, comfort, and natural life exists in the house"
was embodied in her person.[74] And although in the course of
time even Phoebe's spirits came to droop a bit and she was not
as joyful as when she first arrived, yet there was never the
slightest sign of sin in her, no evil in feeling, thought, or action.

The only other resident of the house was a young man by the
name of Holgrave. Poor and in need of a room, he had been
granted the use of one by Hepzibah. He is a daguerreotypist,
which is to say a kind of photographer, although only 22 years
old, but he had already tried several other occupations.
Hepzibah, from the strange types of friends and acquaintances
that he had, thought he must be some kind of a reformer or rev-
olutionist, or at any rate followed "a law of his own." He
showed much interest in the old mansion and knew much about
the history of the Pynchons, including that of Alice Pynchon,
which he told as a story to Phoebe. Surprised at the depth of his
interest Phoebe questioned him about it. He attributed it to his
concern over the great influence exerted by the past over human
lives:

It lies upon the Present like a giant's dead body! In fact, the
case is just as if a young giant were compelled to waste all

his strength in carrying about the corpse of the old giant, his grandfather, who died a long while ago, and only needs to be decently buried. Just think, a moment; and it will startle you to see what slaves we are to bygone times – to Death, if we give the matter the right word![75]

He even condemned the house of the seven gables as an instance of the grip of the past and declared that it "ought to be purified with fire – purified until only its ashes remain." Such being his opinion of the place, Phoebe wondered why he continued to dwell in it. explained:

> Oh, I am pursuing my studies here; not in books however! . . . The house, in my view, is expressive of that odious and abominable Past, with all its bad influences, against which I have just been declaiming. I dwell in it for awhile, that I may know the better how to hate it.[76]

At the time she heard it Phoebe failed to realize its full import, since it was not until later that she learned that was in fact the latest in the line of Old Maule, the wizard, and knew not only the long history of his curse upon the Pynchons, but also possessed something of his wizardry. He possessed powers of hypnotism (or mesmerism).

The influence and weight of the past is heaviest on the person of Judge Jaffrey Pynchon, and it is through his passion and action that the curse achieves its greatest effect and results in a conclusive retribution. In appearance he looked so much like the portrait of the stern old Puritan colonel that still hung on the wall of the study in which he had died that "nobody would doubt that it was "the old Pynchon come again," as Hepzibah said. The judge too was large, portly, wealthy, and the epitome of benign respectability. Yet there was some question whether this was any more than a superficial appearance. Holgrave, who had taken daguerreotypes of the judge, explained his doubts to Phoebe:

Now, the remarkable point is, that the original wears, to the world's eye – and, for aught I know, to his most intimate friends – an exceedingly pleasant countenance, indicative of benevolence, openness of heart, sunny good humor, and other praiseworthy qualities of that cast. The sun, as you see, tells quite another story, and will not be coaxed out of it, after half-a-dozen patient attempts on my part. Here we have the man, sly, subtle, hard, imperious, and, withal, cold as ice. Look at that eye! Would you like to be at its mercy? At that mouth! Could it ever smile? And yet, if you could only see the benign smile of the original![77]

It was the avarice of the judge that initiated the final development of the story of the Pynchons and Maules, a characteristic greed for wealth that he shared with his distant ancestor at the beginning. The judge had used his large influence to obtain the release of Clifford from prison. But he did so not from any benevolence toward his cousin, but in order to have him at his call in the old mansion. From a youthful memory of the time the two shared the same residence the judge was convinced that Clifford possessed the secret regarding the lost deed to the Maine property. To wring that secret out of him, the judge appeared the first day after the prisoner's return at the house of the seven gables. The threat that he was to use against Clifford should he not comply was to have him declared insane and recommitted to an asylum.

Hepzibah opposes the first attempt of the judge, but he seemed determined to force an interview until he heard Clifford calling from the next room and entreating that mercy be shown. The judge feeling that he had erred, withdrew. Yet not for long. He soon reappeared at the house intent upon confronting and threatening Clifford with all the force of his desire. Poor Hepzibah, despite her weakness, stood against him and bitterly denounced him out of fear that the meeting would kill Clifford, declaring:

Why should you do this cruel, cruel thing? – so mad a thing, that I know not whether to call it wicked! Alas,

Cousin Jaffrey, this hard and grasping spirit has run in our blood, these two hundred years. You are but doing over again, in another shape, what your ancestor before you did, and sending down to your posterity the curse inherited from![78]

Finally, convinced that she cannot prevent the judge from getting his way, she asked him to wait while she went to get Clifford and prepared him for the threatening interview. The judge retired to the study and seated himself in the chair where that old Puritan had been found dead, and whose portrait still hung upon the wall. But when Clifford did go to the meeting, he did not find that he had to face a dreaded confrontation. The judge had gone beyond that or any other future interview with him. The judge, like his distant ancestor, was dead in the chair with blood upon his shirt front.

Clifford, although shocked, was overjoyed and exclaimed to his sister, "The weight is gone, Hepzibah; it is gone off this weary old world."[79] Holgrave was affected much the same way when he learned of the death and acknowledged a hereditary interest in the man's life and death. From his knowledge of the family and its history he pointed out the similarity of the judge's death with that of his predecessors and even explained the basis for Old Maule's original curse as based upon a physiological weakness of the whole race of Pynchons.

Consideration of the way in which the judge had died and its resemblance to that of his own uncle also brought out the depth and extent of his sins. It was concluded that in his youth the judge had been far from the exemplary person he pretended to be in later life. He had been something of a scapegrace with pleasures that always left him in want of money, and it was speculated that he had been discovered going through the papers of his uncle, thereby bringing on the death attack. He had then taken advantage of the situation not to deflect the charge of murder from the person of his cousin, Clifford, and allowed the later to be immersed in prison:

> Thus, Jaffrey Pynchon's inward criminality, as regarded
> Clifford, was indeed black and damnable; while it mere
> outward show and positive commission was the smallest
> that could possible consist with so great a sin. This is just
> the sort of guilt that a man of eminent respectability finds it
> easiest to dispose of.[80]

The aftermath of the death brought abundant retribution,
both positive and negative. The judge's only child, a son, had
died abroad even before his father. Thereupon the wealth of the
Pynchons went to Hepzibah, Clifford, and Phoebe, the only
remaining Pynchon, and since she married Holgrave-Maule
also to this last of the Maule's. Negatively, the guilt of the old
Pynchon's from the old Colonel's fraudulent cheating of the first
Maule was brought into the open. That Maule's revenge was
and had been achieved, since as the builder of the house of the
seven gables he had built the hiding place for the long lost deed
to the Maine Lands in a hole behind the Colonel's portrait. This
secret had remained known to the Maule descendants, as young
Holgrave-Maule revealed when he pressed the spring in the
portrait that exposed the hiding place with the decayed and
long useless deed. The Maules had been vindicated. But this
was not true for Clifford. He was too much weakened as a person by his experience in prison. "After such wrong as he had
suffered, there is no reparation."[81] What he needed was love,
and that he was to receive from Hepzibah and Phoebe.

The thesis or moral of the story is emphasized at several
points in the narrative. We are told that:

> The writer cherishes the belief that many, if not most, of the
> successive proprietors of this estate were troubled with
> doubts as to their moral right to hold it . . . If so, we are left
> to dispose of the awful query, whether each inheritor of the
> property, conscious of wrong, and failing to rectify it – did
> not commit anew the great guilt of his ancestor, and incur
> all its original responsibilities. And supposing such to be
> the case, would it not be a far truer mode of expression to

say, of the Pynchon family, that they inherited a great misfortune, than the reverse?[82]

Phoebe on comparing the benevolent presence of the judge with the evil betrayed in the daguerreotype of him, was led to reflect:

> . . . that the hard, stern, relentless look, now on his face, was the same that the sun had so persisted in bringing out. . . . Was it hereditary in him, and transmitted down as a precious heirloom from that bearded ancestor, in whose picture both the expression, and, to a singular degree, the features of the modern Judge, were shown as by a kind of prophecy? A deeper philosopher than Phoebe might have found something very terrible in this idea. It implied that the weaknesses and the defects, the bad passions, the mean tendencies, and the moral diseases which lead to crime, are handed down from one generation to another, by a far surer process of transmission than human law has been able to establish, in respect to the riches and honors which it seeks to entail upon posterity.[83]

We have concentrated attention upon the story of the *House of the Seven Gables*, by singling out the theme of the inheritance of sin. But as we have seen from a previous chapter, that possibility was one of the principal sources of controversy that led to the rise of Unitarianism and to its separation from Congregational Puritanism. The Calvinist Puritans strongly asserted the fact of original sin and its inheritance from generation to generation. The Unitarians denied it. *The House of the Seven Gables* reads as a contribution to that controversy in which it comes down strongly on the side of the Puritans.

The Marble Faun

This romance of the three under our concern is much the most complex in the account that it gives of sin and its effects. It is also more explicit in that it offers an analysis of the development of sin in the moral character of the sinner. The title given to the book on its first publication in England was "Transfigura-tion," and this word identifies its principal theme as "inheri-tance" does the story of the seven gables.

The narrative presents five characters, although one of them, the monk Antonio, serves mainly as the victim of the crime and sin that provides the material of the plot. The two responsible for the crime are Miriam, a beautiful woman, perhaps of a wealthy Jewish family, with a mysterious sin in her past, and Donatello, the Count of Monte Beni, and the last survivor of his ancient Italian family. They have as friends two Americans, Kenyon, a sculptor, and Hilda, a copyist of old masters. Two of these five have mysteries concealed in their past lives, some sin which may have involved both Miriam and Antonio. Donatello and Hilda are both innocent though in different ways, and both have their innocence put to the test. Kenyon is mostly an observ-er of his friends, but both he and Hilda, whom he came to love, fail to meet crucial tests of friendship and in this are guilty of sin. Three of the five are artists living in Rome for the sake of their art, and their interest in each case is centered upon objects concerned with sin.

Miriam, the painter, preferred as subjects Biblical scenes which showed "the idea of woman, acting the part of a revenge-ful mischief towards man."[84] One was a sketch of Jael, wife of a Kenite, driving the nail through the temples of Sisera, thereby ridding Joshua and the Israelites of one of their worst enemies. Another portrayed the triumph of Judith holding the severed head of Holofernes, general-in-chief of the Assyrian army (Judith 13:9–10). Still another showed the daughter of Herodias receiving the head of John the Baptist in a charger (Matt. 14. 8–11). In all the sketches

> The artist's imagination seemed to run on those stories of bloodshed, in which woman's hand was crimsoned by the stain; and how, too – in one from or another, grotesque, or sternly sad-she failed not to bring out the moral, that woman must strike through her own heart to reach a human life, whatever were the motive that impelled her.[85]

Hilda, the copyist, was especially devoted to the painting of Beatrice Cenci by Guido Reni, the young noble woman who was imprisoned and brutally abused by her father, whom she then, with the cooperation of her brothers, murdered and for which she was then executed. To Hilda the painting portrays a girl who is "a fallen angel, and yet sinless; and it is only this depth of sorrow with its weight and darkness, that keeps her down upon the earth." Miriam was not so convinced that it was the portrait of an innocent, and she declared passionately in words that revealed she, Miriam, was much more concerned about sin than Hilda

> Ah,. . . if I could only get within her consciousness! If I could but clasp Beatrice's ghost and draw it to myself! I would give my life to know whether she thought herself innocent, or the one great criminal since time began.[86]

Kenyon's preferred choice of subject for sculpture was not as indicative of his character as that of the women. His statue of Cleopatra was that of a beautiful, fierce, and passionate woman in repose, but a repose of despair. Miriam on beholding it for the first time was suddenly moved to tell Kenyon of the secret that lay on her conscience. She also passionately appealed to him. But she detected in him at once an alarm and even a withdrawal that completely stopped her, and she condemned him, saying, "You are as cold and pitiless as your own marble."[87]

Donatello is the central person of the story. His is the crime that motivates the action involving all his friends. His is the transformation that is greater than that of any of the others. To the artists he is seen as a living image of the marble fawn sculpted by Praxiteles. Not only in looks was he likened to the Italian god of the fields, but also in actions and even in personality. To Miriam, whom he loved, he gave

> the idea of a being not precisely man, nor yet a child, but in a high and beautiful sense, an animal; a creature in a state of development less than what mankind has attained, yet the more perfect within itself for that very deficiency.[88]

Donatello in turn was quick to respond to every mood of Miriam's, whether of joy or sorrow or terror.

The sin or crime hidden in her past returned to torment, even to terrorize, Miriam upon the appearance in Rome of a mysterious and ominous man who had been associated somehow with her in that event. In Rome this Antonio lived as a Capuchin monk. Yet he managed to follow Miriam continually, much to her discomfort, and she had been quite despaired of ever ridding herself of his presence. Donatello, who sensed her feelings, provided Miriam with the release that she desired. One night the four friends while out for a stroll found themselves on the Capitoline Hill at the site of the Tarpeian Rock, the place where those convicted of treason to the Roman Republic were cast over the cliff to their death. There Miriam and Donatello lingered after Kenyon and Hilda had gone on. There also, as they became aware, was the dreaded Antonio. Donatello, with scarcely more than a thought, treated him as the old Romans had their guilty traitor by flinging him over the cliff. Miriam in horror, asked him what he had done, and Donatello replied: "I did what your eyes bade me do, when I asked them with mine, as I held the wretch over the precipice!"[89] And Miriam:

> She turned to him – the guilty, blood-stained lonely woman – she turned to her fellow-criminal, the youth, so lately innocent, whom she had drawn into her doom. . . . "Yes, Donatello, you speak the truth!" said she. "My heart consented to what you did. We two slew yonder wretch. The deed knots us together for time and eternity, like to coil of a serpent!!"[90]

Almost immediately transformations began to occur in all the characters. Indeed, the passage just quoted comes at the beginning of a chapter entitled "The Faun's Transformation." The death deprived Donatello of his sunny nature and wonted merriment, and he declared that he would never be happy again. Although the crime had brought him and Miriam closer together than ever before, the woman recognized that her friend's anguish could only be alleviated, if never forgotten, by their separating and not seeing one another. Donatello departed from Rome and retired to his ancestral home in the Tuscan hills outside of Florence.

Unbeknown to the two, Hilda had witnessed the commission of their crime. She was entirely overwhelmed at the horror of it and in her room shed tears from the sorrow that "the innocent heart pours forth, at its first actual discovery that sin is in the world." The narrator remarks upon this occurrence:

> The young and pure are not apt to find out that miserable truth, until it is brought home to them by the guiltiness of some trusted friend. They may have heard much of the evil of the world, and seem to know it but only as an impalpable theory. In due time, some mortal, whom they reverence too highly, is commissioned by Providence to teach them this direful lesson; he perpetuates a sin; and Adam falls anew, and Paradise, heretofore in unfaded bloom, is lost again.[91]

Hilda also then experienced her first personal fall in her relation with Miriam. The latter had come in the disturbance of her feeling to her best friend for comfort and relief. But she is repulsed by Hilda, who wanted never to see or meet her again. The girl then revealed that she had witnessed the murder and at the moment that it occurred had seen in her friend's eyes "a look of hatred, triumph, vengeance, and, as it were, joy at some unhoped for relief!"[92] Yet she promised to keep that knowledge a secret, even though she expected to be tormented in mind by it as though she was herself the guilty one. Hilda declared:

> Ah, now I understand how the sins of generations past have created an atmosphere of sin for those that follow! While there is a single guilty person in the universe, each innocent one must feel his innocence tortured by that guilt. Your deed, Miriam, has darkened the whole sky![93]

And in the days that followed she sank into a deep despondency.

Kenyon soon learned that all three of his friends had come into deep trouble. They ceased to be at all companionable and seemed to have lost all interest in life. To seek a needed change he acted upon Donatello's invitation and went to visit him in the Tuscan hills at Monte Beni. However, the only change he found in his young friend was that he acted as though he bore thirty years of sin and was deeply melancholy and in need of penitence. He could not stand any mention of Miriam and trembled with anger and terror at the mere sound of her name. Formerly the young count had lived at harmony with nature and readily attracted wild birds and animals to him. But that power had left him, and he attributed its loss to the shadow that had covered him.

Miriam had left Rome, and Kenyon discovered that she had visited Monte Beni, although without seeing Donatello: Kenyon met her secretly and found her a shadow of her former joyous self. She had come hoping to find a way in which she might help Donatello. But she was afraid and dared not approach him, for she knew that he had a horror of her. Kenyon welcomed her warmly and received her move toward confidence without rejecting it as he had in Rome. He told her it was his belief that Donatello still loved her and sought to explain that he believed that some calamity had shocked the count into a state of misery, pain, and repugnance along with the desire to do penance. But now he was coming out of that state and "out of bitter agony, a soul and intellect . . . have been inspired into him."[94] If that is so Miriam believed that she might be of some help, no matter what sacrifice it might cost. Kenyon agreed and drew up a plan which would make it possible for Donatello and Miriam to meet.

They did meet, and the meeting was successful as Kenyon had hoped it would be. Donatello spoke to Miriam, and she knew from his words that he still loved her. More than that:

That tone, too, bespoke an altered and deepened character; it told of a vivified intellect, and of spiritual instruction that had come through sorrow and remorse; so that – instead of the wild boy, the thing of sportive, animal nature, the sylvan Faun – here was now the man of feeling and intelligence.[95]

Miriam and Donatello then agreed that their life henceforth would be together, but rather by way of penance than for any earthly happiness.

Hilda in Rome remained lonely and desolate, tormented by the guilty secret that she had promised not to reveal, thereby made more wretched by having to contain it inside herself. Her sorrow changed her appearance, and she began to resemble more her favorite portrait, that of Beatrice Cenci. In extreme anguish she wandered into St. Peter's Cathedral, where she observed a penitent emerging from a confessional box with an expression of relief and peace on her face. So moved and although not a Catholic, Hilda herself entered a confessional and freed herself of the awful secret.

> And, ah, what a relief! When they hysteric gasp, the strife between words and sobs, had subsided, what a torture had passed away from her soul! It was all gone, her bosom was as pure now as in her childhood. She was a girl again.[96]

But not in every way the same girl she had been before she has witnessed the crime. She was able to return to her customary activity, but was not so perfect as a copyist. "She could not yield herself up to the painter so unreservedly as in time past; her character had developed a sturdier quality, which made her less pliable to the influence of other minds."[97] She saw beauty less acutely and responded less to it, but "she felt truth, or the lack of it profoundly."[98] She also questioned the rightness of her action towards her former friend Miriam.

> It was not that the deed looked less wicked and terrible, in the retrospect; but she asked herself whether there were not other questions to be considered, aside from that single one

of Miriam's guilt or innocence; as, for example, whether a close bond of friendship, in which we once voluntarily engage, ought to be severed on account of any unworthiness, which we subsequently detect in our friend.[99]

Thus upon Hilda no less than upon Miriam the crime and sin committed against the monk effected transformations in their characters that were all to the good.

However, it is the change and transformation wrought in the character of Donatello that was most noted and remarked upon. Once Kenyon saw the count some time after his reconciliation with Miriam, it seemed that "some of the sweet and delightful characteristics of the antique Faun had reappeared." Miriam agreed, declaring:

> So changed, yet still, in a deeper sense, so much the same! He has travelled in a circle, as all things heavenly and earthly do, and now comes back to his original self, with an inestimable treasure of improvement won from an experience of pain. . . . Was the crime – in which he and I were wedded – was it a blessing in that strange disguise? Was it a means of education, bringing a simple and imperfect nature to a point of feeling and intelligence, which it could have reached under no other discipline? . . . this great mystery. . . . The story of the Fall of Man! Is it not repeated in our Romance of Monte Beni? And may we follow the analogy yet farther? Was that very sin – into which Adam precipitated himself and all his race – was it the destined means by which, over a long path-way of toil and sorrow, we are to attain a higher, brighter, and profounder happiness, than our lost birthright gave? Will not this idea account for the permitted existence of sin, as no other theory can?[100]

This theory repeats that expressed in the phrase *felix culpa* of the old Roman Catholic liturgy of Holy Week that the sin of Adam was a "happy fault" since it brought to earth the Redeemer with a still greater future for human kind. But Miriam's words provide no indication at all of any reference to Jesus Christ.

Kenyon in conversation with Hilda took upon again the idea put forth by Miriam about Donatello's development:

> He perpetrated a great crime; and his remorse, gnawing into his soul, has awakened it; developing a thousand high capabilities, moral and intellectual, which we never should have dreamed of asking for, within the scanty compass of the Donatello whom we knew. . . . Sin has educated Donatello, and elevated him. Is Sin, then – which we deem such a dreadful blackness in the universe – is it, like Sorrow, merely an element of human education, through which we struggle to a higher and purer state than we could otherwise have attained. Did Adam fall, that we might rise to a far loftier Paradise than his?[101]

Hilda repudiated strongly any such theory, claiming that it makes a mockery of religion and mortality and annuls the precepts of heaven. Yet she did not deny that sin had as a result, if not as a cause, the transformation in the moral character not only of Donatello, but also of Miriam as well as herself.

Endnotes

1   "Fancy's Show Box" in *Tales*, p. 450.

2   "The Snow-Image" in *Tales*, Preface, p. 1154.

3   "Fancy's Show Box," p. 452.

4   *Ibid.*, p. 453.

5   *Ibid.*, pp. 454–55.

6   *Ibid.*, p. 455.

7   *Ibid.*, p. 454.

8   *Ibid.*, p. 455.

9   "Egotism; or the Bosom-Serpent" in *Tales*, p. 793.

10   *Ibid.*, p. 794.

11   *Ibid.*, p. 793.

12   "The Christmas Banquet" in *Tales*, p. 867.

13   "Ethan Brand" in *Tales*, p. 1056.

14   *Ibid.*, p. 1057.

15   *Ibid.*, p. 1064.

16   "The Man of Adamant" in *Tales*, p. 428.

17 "Earth's Holocaust" in *Tales*, p. 905.

18 *Ibid.*, p. 906.

19 "Young Goodman Brown" in *Tales*, p. 287.

20 *The Scarlet Letter* in *Novels*, p. 175.

21 *Ibid.*, p. 176.

22 *Ibid.*, p. 169.

23 *Ibid.*, p. 171.

24 *Ibid.*, p. 182.

25 *Ibid.*, p. 183.

26 *Ibid.*, p. 184.

27 *Ibid.*, p. 187.

28 *Ibid.*

29 *Ibid.*, p. 190.

30 *Ibid.*, pp. 192–93.

31 *Ibid.*, p. 194.

32 *Ibid.*, p. 227.

33 *Ibid.*, p. 227.

34 *Ibid.*, p. 230.

35 *Ibid.*, p. 232.

36 *Ibid.*, p. 234.

37 *Ibid.*, pp. 235–36.

38 *Ibid.*, p. 237.

39 *Ibid.*, p. 238.

40 *Ibid.*, p. 240.

41 *Ibid.*, p. 242.

42 *Ibid.*, p. 243.

43 *Ibid.*, p. 250.

44 *Ibid.*, p. 253.

45 *Ibid.*, p. 257.

46 *Ibid.*, p. 261.

47 *Ibid.*

48 *Ibid.*, p. 264.

49 *Ibid.*, p. 266.

50 *Ibid.*

51 *Ibid.*, p. 267.

52 *Ibid.*, p. 268.

53 *Ibid.*, p. 270.

54 *Ibid.*, p. 274.

55 *Ibid.*, p. 283.

56 *Ibid.*, p. 286.

57 *Ibid.*, pp. 337–38.

58 *Ibid.*, p. 339.

59 *Ibid.*, pp. 258–59.

60 *Ibid.*, pp. 342–43.

61 *The House of the Seven Gables* in *Novels*, p. 352.

62 *Ibid.*, p. 358.

63 *Ibid.*, p. 367.

64 *Ibid.*, p. 533.

65 *Ibid.*, pp. 530–31.

66 *Ibid.*, p. 370.

67 *Ibid.*, p. 421.

68 *Ibid.*, p. 466.

69 *Ibid.*, p. 445.

70 *Ibid.*, p. 442.

71 *Ibid.*, p. 468.

72 *Ibid.*, p. 458.

73 *Ibid.*, pp. 453–54.

74 *Ibid.*, p. 538.

75 *Ibid.*, p. 509.

76 *Ibid.*, p. 510.

77 *Ibid.*, p. 431.

78 *Ibid.*, p. 556.

79 *Ibid.*, p. 566.

80 *Ibid.*, p. 621.

81 *Ibid.*

82 *Ibid.*, p. 368.

83 *Ibid.*, p. 454.

84 *The Marble Fawn* in *Novels*, p. 888.

85 *Ibid.*

86 *Ibid.*, pp. 906–7.

87   *Ibid.*, p. 960.

88   *Ibid.*, p. 916,

89   *Ibid.*, p. 996.

90   *Ibid.*, p. 997.

91   *Ibid.*, pp. 1021–22.

92   *Ibid.*, p. 1026.

93   *Ibid.*, p. 1028.

94   *Ibid.*, p. 1087.

95   *Ibid.*, p. 1119.

96   *Ibid.*, p. 1149.

97   *Ibid.*, p. 1164.

98   *Ibid.*, p. 1133.

99   *Ibid.*, p. 1173.

100   *Ibid.*, pp. 1214–15.

101   *Ibid.*, p. 1236.

On Hawthorne's Position

We have now considered many of the writings of Hawthorne that bear upon religion and its beliefs and only what the writings themselves say. Nor have we attempted to identify what they have to say about these subjects with the narrator, let alone with the man writing their narrative. Yet lest we leave that man in some kind of limbo without hazarding a word about his own position, it seems only honest that something should be said on our part of what we think that Hawthorne's position might have been.

But to do so is to run a risk that so far we have tried to avoid. To take the words of writers of fiction and to attribute them as propositions to the person who writes them is based upon a large assumption. At its most simplistic, it presupposes that writers are always expressing their own heartfelt beliefs. But such an assumption supposes that writers write only out of their heart, their deepest beliefs as persons, and not at all out of imagination regarding what the story requires. This assumption supposes that a fictional character never captures its author and takes on a life of its own. And we know, at least from writers who tell about their own experience of writing, that often happens.

Worse than that, to suppose that writers' fiction is always a transcript of their own life's experiences denigrates if it does not deny the productive and creative powers of the poetic imagination.

In Hawthorne's case, the double-dealing involved in equat-
ing the words of the writer with the beliefs of the man writing
are easily exposed. In the *Scarlet Letter* the action of Hester and
Dimmesdale is presented as a crime and a sin and acknowledged as such by Hester as well as by Dimmesdale. However, in
the scene in the woods where the two meet and again express
their love, with Hester claiming that it is more sacred than any
relation she ever had with Chillingworth, she in effect revokes
the first statement. Now if we want to identify the sentiments
expressed with Hawthorne the man, which of the two statements represents the position of the writer? It is ridiculous and
contrary to the artistry of the writer to identify the man's personal position with one or the other. The position in each case is
true to the imagined story. And if Hester's later position here is
truer to some of those taken in the 19th century than those of the
first as belonging to the Puritan period, there is still an assumption to be made to suppose that those of Hawthorne side with
that of the 19th century.

However, this much said about the dangers, is it impossible
to say anything at all about the position of Hawthorne the man
behind the writing regarding the issues that we have considered? Not necessarily. For there is a way of mitigating, if not of
entirely avoiding, the error of identifying the words of the narrator with those of the man writing as such. The writings, as we
have seen, express clear, definite, and strong opinions about certain issues involving religion. Much is also known about the circle of acquaintances in which Hawthorne moved in mid-19th
century Massachusetts. By his writings and especially by his
marriage with Sophia Peabody, Hawthorne came to know and
be known and to move among the intellectual leaders of that
group.

Indeed, it is not too much to claim that he knew all the principal apostles: the apostle of Transcendentalism – Emerson; of
Unitarianism – Channing; of public schooling – Horace Mann;
of Kindergarten schools – Elizabeth Peabody; and of the
Abolition of slavery – all of the above.

Hawthorne's acquaintance with these various individuals, even if he never was intimate with them, owed mostly to the influence of his wife Sophia Peabody. The Peabody women were a moving force in Boston society, and among the earliest glories of the feminist movement. Elizabeth, the oldest of the Peabody daughters, organized a center not only of feminist intellectualism but also of Transcendentalism and of the abolitionist movement for the freedom of the slaves. She knew Emerson well and had been his pupil; she was the student, follower, and secretary of Channing, apostle of Unitarianism. The younger sister Mary became the wife of Horace Mann, the apostle of non-sectarian public school education and, after his death, the founder of a school for children.

Nathaniel after his marriage came to know all of these prominent people. His sister-in-law Elizabeth helped him to publish his earliest writings. Through her friendship with Emerson and Channing, she became one of the first members of the Transcendental Club and was devoted to promoting the doctrines of German Idealism. With the support of Channing she opened the West Street Book Shop that became a center of Boston intellectuals.

Horace Mann, the apostle of non-sectarian public schools, was the brother-in-law of Hawthorne. Both of the Manns, as well as Elizabeth Peabody, were strong advocates of public schooling, i.e., schooling outside of the home. Indeed, all three are now remembered and lauded as founders and heroes of public-school education. But their position must have made for disagreements and hard feelings with the Hawthornes. Both Nathaniel and Sophia maintained that their children had to be educated at home. For if they were allowed to attend an outside school, they would be corrupted. The Hawthornes maintained their belief, against their relatives, the Manns, that educating children at home was the best way.[1]

Channing as already noted, was the apostle of Unitarianism. Elizabeth as his secretary had copied out some 50 of his earliest sermons so that they could be published. Thus Elizabeth,

Hawthorne's sister-in-law, helped to promote the first successes of Unitarianism.

From what we know of Hawthorne from comments on his relatives in his journals and in his letters to his wife, Hawthorne's relations with these eminent and influential men must have been strained on occasion, as were those of his wife Sophia. Emerson, the seer of Transcendentalism, was a close neighbor; while both families lived in Concord Hawthorne surely met him frequently. Yet all the documentary evidence shows that the two men never became close friends, and never got on well together. When they met, Emerson talked a lot, Hawthorne listened a lot. Sophia, after she married, thought little of Emerson, since "he knows not much of love."[2] Emerson is reported to have never been able to finish reading any of Hawthorne's writings. Yet he declared his strong dislike for *The Blithedale Romance* and called *The Marble Faun* so much "mush."[3]

With Horace Mann, Hawthorne's relations must have been strained perhaps much of the time. The two men were vastly different in personality, outlook and interests. Horace Mann was a temperance man; Hawthorne enjoyed his glass of wine. Mann was an abolitionist, strongly opposed to slavery, and hence also to the candidacy of Franklin Pierce for the presidency of the United States; Pierce opposed immediate emancipation. Hawthorne was a close friend of Pierce's from his college days till his death. Hawthorne wrote a successful, and laudatory, monograph about his friend when he ran for U.S. President. Mann was also president of Antioch College in Ohio and had begot trouble for himself by inviting his Unitarian friends from the East to lecture there. Accordingly, Hawthorne disagreed with his brother-in-law on a host of matters. To illustrate his rigidity, Horace Mann on one occasion finding Hawthorne smoking a cigar declared that he could no longer hold the man in such a high regard as he had.

Hawthorne in marrying Sophia Peabody had entry into the intellectual life of Boston Society. Yet given Hawthorne's preference for solitude and withdrawing into his immediate family, there also must have been strains: strain brought about by the way in which he drew his wife away from the influence of her sisters and their beliefs and those of their friends.

Hawthorne and his wife may well have had disagreements. But there were also agreements between them, agreements that came to set Sophia against both of her sisters, Elizabeth and Mary. For example: those two sisters remained strong supporters of Emerson and the Transcendentalist doctrine, of Channing and his Unitarianism, of the public schooling promoted by Horace Mann, and of the strong opposition to slavery espoused by the northern abolitionists. Disagreement over the issue of slavery became so great that it almost led to an open break between the sisters. Elizabeth continued to write long letters on the subject to Sophia in which she defended the right of breaking the laws regarding fugitive slaves, which led Sophia to write in reply: "I consider it a very dangerous and demoralizing doctrine and have always called it 'transcendental slang.' . . . I am just on the point of declaring that I hate transcendentalism because it is full of such immoderate dicta."[4] Furthermore at one point Hawthorne refused to give Elizabeth's letters to Sophia, on the grounds that they would only upset her to no good end.[5]

The three sisters also held differences regarding Unitarianism and a more liberal Christianity than that of the old Puritans. Hawthorne may not have himself held the Puritan beliefs. Yet his writings expressed positions opposed to the newer doctrines. These read in the light of the parody, "The Celestial Rail-road," could be likened to those of Mr. Smooth-it-away in desiring an easier Christianity.

As we have already seen, the doctrine of original sin and its inheritance was a highly controversial topic in Hawthorne's day. Emerson, Channing, and Mann objected strongly to sin being inherited from one generation to the next. Hawthorne's *The House of Seven Gables* carries as a principal theme the inheritance of sin and guilt and its disastrous effects. All three men were Transcendentalist advocates of social and moral reform and believers in its efficacy. Yet some of Hawthorne's tales and especially *The Blithedale Romance* express sharp criticism of the idealized fervor for reform as illusionary and mistaken.

It is not surprising then that Emerson could not read the writings of Hawthorne. Emerson disbelieved and repudiated opinions expressed in them as attacks upon some of his dearest and deepest beliefs. Much the same could be said also of Emerson's friends Channing and Mann.

Hawthorne wrote at some length about the books of religion left in the Old Manse, the house in Concord where he and his new wife lived from 1842 to 1845. This library contained works of the old orthodoxy as well as some of the more recent liberal sort, among the latter the Unitarian bimonthly *The Examiner* and *The Liberal Preacher*. On comparing the two, Hawthorne in his *American Notebook*, expressed a sharper judgment in favor of the older than he did in the version published in the preface to *Mosses from an Old Manse*.[6]

> Doctor Ripley's own additions to the library are not of a very interesting character. Volumes of the Christian Examiner and Liberal Preacher, modern sermons, the controversial works of Unitarian ministers, and all such trash; but which, I suppose, express fairly enough, when compared with the elder portion of the library, the difference between the cold, lifeless, vaguely liberal clergyman of our own day, and the narrow but earnest cushion-thumper of puritanical times. On the whole, I prefer the last-mentioned variety of the black-coated tribe.[7]

Such disagreement and opposition suggests a hypothesis that could account for a side of Hawthorne's personality that has long enthralled his critics. Hawthorne was famous during his own lifetime, and perhaps even more since his death, for his shyness, his reticence, and the fact that as a young man he had been for many years a recluse. This trait of his has given rise, especially to the delight of his psychobiographers, to the theory that he must have had a secret that he was intent upon concealing, probably because it had a sexual root. Hence, it is argued, he was quiet and retired from fear that he might inadvertently reveal it.

However, there remains another possibility. The reclusivity of Hawthorne as a young man may have had many causes, causes that God alone knows. For his reticence within the close circle of the writers just mentioned there may well be another reason. Hawthorne was reluctant to talk about his beliefs with Emerson, Channing, and Mann, not because he had nothing to say about the matters they were interested in, but because his position on those matters was radically different from theirs. He did not enjoy controversy; he preferred to keep silent; he staked out the position that he was interested in investigating in his tales and novels. There they became public property available to any reader.

Endnotes

1   T. Walter Herbert, Dearest Beloved: *The Hawthornes and the Making of the Middle Class Family* (Berkeley: University of California Press, 1993), xix, pp. 172–74.

2   *Ibid.*, p. 189.

3   E. H. Miller, *Salem Is My Dwelling Place: A Life of Nathaniel Hawthorne* (Iowa City: Iowa University Press, 1991), pp. 215, 367, and 447.

4   Louise Hall Tharp, *The Peabody Sisters of Salem* (London: George G. Harrap and Co., 1951; Boston: Little, Brown and Co., 1988), p. 246.

5   *Ibid.*, p. 245.

6   *Mosses from an Old Manse* in *Tales*, pp. 1135–38.

7   Nathaniel Hawthorne, *The American Notebooks*, The Centenary Edition, Vol. VIII (Columbus: Ohio State University Press, 1972), Tuesday, August 16th, 1842, p. 7.

Part 3
The Catholic Saint

Rose Hawthorne
Lathrop

Mother Alphonsa

The Life and Achievement of Rose Hawthorne Lathrop: Mother Alphonsa

The religious legacy Nathaniel Hawthorne inherited from his Puritan ancestors continued to cast its influence in two distinct ways long after his death. The first, and better known, is through Nathaniel's short stories, his romances and his journals. Today classrooms and libraries throughout the world recognize Hawthorne as a major figure in American literature. The Bowdoin College library in Maine attests to this with its bibliographical index on Hawthorne that runs to more than 800 entries, including his novels, short stories, essays and journals along with numerous scholars' biographies and critical commentary.

The second way Nathaniel Hawthorne's religious influence continued to be felt has received much less public attention: through his children, especially his daughters, Una and Rose. Nathaniel's children walked paths strikingly different from their famous father – and yet all were clearly allied to their father and his spirit. This topic is the focus of the current section. In taking it up, there are two aspects to explore. One has to do with the kind of religious affiliations Nathaniel's daughters made. The second is the form of career – life's work – that they took up.

The story of how and why Nathaniel Hawthorne's daughters made the choices they did is as filled with unexpected twists as any of their famous father's romances. The work started by Rose carries on yet today through the series of six hospital-nursing homes she founded to care for destitute cancer victims and through the religious order of sisters she founded, the Dominican Sisters of Hawthorne. Their headquarters is at Rosary Hill in Hawthorne, New York. Rose herself lived in earlier incarnations of Rosary Hill from 1901 until her death in 1926.

Una was the first of Hawthorne's children, the child born of the extended honeymoon period Nathaniel and his wife Sophia enjoyed after their 1842 marriage when he was thirty eight. They were living a secluded life at the Old Manse in Concord, Massachusetts, at the time of Una's birth. A much-desired child, Una was born in 1844 following Sophia's 1843 miscarriage. Some time after Una's birth the family had to go without the services of a maid because of their meager financial resources. To spare the uncertain health of his wife, Hawthorne took on himself many of the cooking and cleaning tasks of the little house, as Sophia reports on lovingly in letters to her father.[1]

The Hawthorne family rejoiced in the birth of their son, Julian, in 1846, two years after Una's birth. Their last child, Rose, was born in 1851, apparently to considerably less fanfare. "Nathaniel greeted Rose's arrival as something as an anticlimax," a biographer of Rose noted. It took Nathaniel two months to announce Rose's birth, in a single brief paragraph, in a long letter to his sister Louisa.[2] On the other hand Nathaniel wrote in a letter to a friend, "I think I feel more interest in her than I did in the other children at the same age, from consideration that she is the daughter of my age, the comfort (at least to be hoped) of my declining years."[3]

The first two years of Rose's life coincided with a period of enormous literary productivity for Hawthorne. He published *The House of Seven Gables* in 1851, then *A Wonder Book for Girls and Boys*. Between December 1851 and April 1852, he wrote *The Blithedale Romance*; in the fall of 1852 he wrote *The Life of Franklin Pierce*, a presidential campaign biography for his college chum who was elected the fourteenth President of the United States. In 1853 he published *The Tanglewood Tales for Girls and Boys.*

In 1853 the Hawthorne family left their familiar New England surroundings to move to England, where Nathaniel served as consul in Liverpool. The position, one of the few permanent full-time positions Hawthorne held during his life, was a political appointment, arranged through the offices of President Franklin Pierce.

Because of her father's increased responsibilities away from home, Rose enjoyed less of his companionship than her brother and sister, and she felt the poorer for this. Rose notes in her 1897 memoir of her father that unlike her sister and her brother, her knowledge of her father was "trivial and meager" since he died the day before her thirteenth birthday. She wrote she never "was allowed to grow, as I wished, out of the appellations of Rosebud, Baby, and Babs, as my father always called me." Instead, she added, she "had to be satisfied with a glance and a smile, which was so much less than he had been able to give my brother and sister in their happier childhood days."[4]

Still, in common with the rest of her family who committed their memories of Hawthorne for publication, Rose idealized her father. She remembered him as a towering, almost too-good-to-be true figure, the center of the family's existence. "I always felt in awe of him, a tremendous sense of his power . . .", she said. "And he, I was fully aware, could see through me as easily as if I were a soul in one of his own books." Rose also said her father gave her "a sense of having a great ally among the great ones of life." If she was ill, he stood by her bed, as if to defy illness itself. And she recalled him as a talented gift-giver: "All his presents were either unusual or of exquisite workmanship. The fairy quality was indispensable before he chose them."[5]

The early years in the Hawthorne household, as the children began to grow up, were marked by love and affection and consideration for others, especially the most needy, as Rose and her brother Julian recalled years later. The family apparently did not attend formal religious services or instruction. According to her letters to her father and mother from Liverpool, England, Sophia took the children to formal religious services at Chester Cathedral, one of the great old Anglican cathedrals. She added that it was exactly the kind of church she wanted for their first formal exposure to Christianity in church.[6] The children remained unbaptized until 1857 during their sojourn in England. William Henry Channing, a former acquaintance of the Hawthorne family in New England and recently called as pastor to the Renshaw Street Chapel, baptized the three children into the Unitarian Church. Sophia noted that she often attended the services at the chapel, since she held Channing's sermons in high regard.[7]

At the same time, the Hawthornes nurtured their children's religious sensitivities as Christians in a number of crucial, informal ways. In Concord, the family's visitors included Transcendentalists such as Emerson and Bronson Alcott and Unitarians such as William Henry Channing; they often discussed religious concepts and the tenets of a moral life.

At least some of the time Hawthorne led his family and servant in prayers on Sunday, as he did in Liverpool. In addition, the symbols of religion surrounded the family and could be seen in the portraits hanging in prominent positions in their living room and study at the Wayside. One favorite, a gift from Ralph Waldo Emerson, was of the artist Raphael's Transfiguration. Another, hung in a place of honor, was a portrait of the Madonna and Child by Corregio.[8]

Despite the lack of formal religious education, for the Hawthorne family, what made up a moral life was part of the air they breathed wherever they lived. Sophia, following the example of her mother and sisters and the Unitarians in general, saw religion in practical as well as intellectual terms. To introduce her children to the concept of serving others, she often took them with her while she visited sick neighbors.

In addition, though money was a chronic problem for the

family, Sophia taught her children by her example that whatever they had was to be shared with others. In Liverpool, for example, Christmas was celebrated with small gifts for the Hawthorne children but also with putting together packets for the poor.

The children received other informal instruction on the importance of religion as well. Sophia taught Sunday school on occasion. And she and Nathaniel read to their children from the Bible and tales with a strong religious theme such as *Pilgrim's Progress*. In addition, the Hawthornes taught their children to respect people's beliefs through their friendship with people of diverse religious convictions. A friend of Sophia's, Mrs. Sam Ward, converted to Catholicism, as did a niece of Emerson's, who went on to become a Visitation nun. As a child, a Catholic friend of the family introduced Rose to St. Rose of Lima as her patron saint.

Nathaniel Hawthorne played his part as well. In an 1850 letter, Sophia told her mother a story to illustrate the way Nathaniel encouraged his children to think about moral behavior. On this one occasion, at least, he held Jesus as a model for them to follow. Paraphrasing Sophia's story, the incident goes as follows:

> At the children's request, Sophia was reading a story about Jesus. In the midst of the story, Una got up to get something. Julian immediately claimed her seat as his own. Una complained, "Julian, you can't do that! It isn't fair to take my place just because I just get up for a minute!" At this juncture, their father spoke up saying: "Una, what do you think Jesus would have said, if he were in your place? In the Bible, Jesus teaches the disciples how they are to give to those who need help, 'If a man take your cloak, give him your coat also.' What do you think that means, Una?" Nathaniel's words had an immediate effect on Una, causing her to stop complaining and relinquishing her seat to her brother.[9]

Another incident Sophia views as an indication of her husband's implicit Christian faith (and one of his most important legacies) is Nathaniel's compassion in embracing the child with leprosy in England. In a letter written shortly after his death, Sophia says about the event: "Was that not divine! Was it not Christianity in one action – what a bequest to his children – what a new revelation of Christ to the world was that!"[10]

Other Hawthorne relatives also impressed the children with the strength of their religious fervor. From their Aunt Elizabeth Peabody, the young Hawthornes may well have learned what it meant to be an advocate for a religion. A disciple of Channing, Elizabeth did her considerable best to promote Channing's religious and philosophical beliefs.

From Sophia especially, the children learned what it meant to take an active role in service to others. From Nathaniel, they learned to look beyond ordinary events to see their larger value or significance.

The historical record points to the conclusion, then, that though their formal religious education was minimal, the three children grew up surrounded by religious concepts and practices and aware that their parents, other family members and friends placed a high value on religious principles and moral ways of behaving.

The period in Italy was another influential source of information about religion for the three children, perhaps especially for Rose. According to what she writes much later, the year and a half in Italy following the four years in Liverpool were important ones. Since Rose was so young, less than ten, when the family returned to their Wayside home in the United States in 1860, it can't be said with any certainty that her life's direction as a Catholic and a nun were set during the European adventure. Still, it is possible to say that as impressionable and sensitive children the three Hawthorne siblings were exposed to the grand sweep of Catholicism in Italy's magnificent churches and cathedrals. And as commentators on the experience, the young

Hawthornes had a mother with a trained artist's eye and a father who was open to and sensitive to the religious impulse and experience in Italy. Due especially to their mother's keen interest in art, the family frequently visited museums to absorb the art. Many were of a religious nature, imparting to viewers some knowledge of church tradition as told through art masterpieces.

Rose also tells repeatedly the story of running as a small child in the gardens of the Vatican and bumping into the pope, known in Italian as Pio Nino. Perhaps charmed by the lively little girl with the red curls, he blessed her and patted her on the head.

The servants during the Hawthorne's time in Italy were Catholics; this gave the children first-hand experience of home-based religious practice. Living in Florence while her father was beginning *The Marble Faun*, Rose later recalled that she frequently observed a young servant girl kneeling down in prayer. And a biographer tells the tale how an Italian servant in Florence gave Rose an infant of wax, sleeping in flowers under a glass case and how Rose came to feel that the Christ Child loved her all the time, even in her sleep.

In the churches and on the roads in the Italian cities, the Hawthorne family often passed shrines on their sightseeing tours, which Hawthorne spoke approvingly of:

> Whatever may be the iniquities of the papal system, it was a wise and lovely sentiment that set up frequent shrine and cross along the roadside. No wayfarer, bent on whatever worldly errand can fail to be reminded, at every mile or two, that this is not the business which most concerns him. . . . the pleasureseeker . . . the wretch in temptation . . . the stubborn criminal.[11]

While on their sightseeing tours in Italy, the Hawthornes also often encountered groups of priests, monks, and nuns. Though Hawthorne was strongly anti-clerical, as was Sophia, he was more appreciative of the lives led by religious women. He spoke at times with grudging approval of the kind of life nuns led.

As children and adults, the Hawthornes could look into their father's books and journals and into their mother's many letters to friends and family members to get an idea of their impressions of Europe and Catholicism. Rose, for instance, wrote that she made it a point to read all of her father's writings at fifteen except *The Scarlet Letter*. She put this romance off until eighteen, writing that she had been told its subject matter was too sophisticated for a younger girl.[12]

In Nathaniel's journals and in the novel, *The Marble Faun*, Hawthorne's children could see his interest in and appreciation for at least part of Catholicism's rich heritage. He displays a keen interest in the sacrament of penance, for instance, noting how telling their sins to a priest brings Catholics a sense of forgiveness and peace. In *The Marble Faun*, Hilda, who describes herself as a "daughter of the Puritans" through and through, nonetheless enters a confessional and pours out her heart to a priest, telling him of her horror at inadvertently witnessing Donatello push Miriam's persecutor off a parapet to his death. The result, as described in the book by Hilda's friend Kenyon, was a

> transfiguration – a marvelous change from the sad girl who had entered the confessional, bewildered with anguish, to this bright, yet softened, image of religious consolation that emerged from it. It was as if one of the throng of angelic people, who might be hovering in the sunny depths of the Dome, had alighted on the pavement.[13]

An unhappy part of the Hawthorne family's Italian visit was the lengthy illness Una suffered during their year and a half in Rome and Italy. Una became seriously ill with what was popularly called the "Roman fever" (most likely, malaria) and lingered on precariously ill and sometimes close to death for many months. The illness left her with a tendency to frail health and apparently to mental instability and breakdowns. During this

time, Nathaniel and Sophia proved themselves devoted attendants, staying persistently by Una's bedside and doing all they
could to tempt her back to good health.

For the other children, the illness was a strain, a cloud on
their European journey. As Nathaniel's notebooks for the period
indicate that during Una's illness, the life of the entire family
revolved around Una and her needs. Her frail health remained
a source of concern from this time on, as Julian noted in a biography of Hawthorne: "The least mischance to Una wrung her
father's heart."[14]

A researcher into Rose Hawthorne and her relationship to
her family maintains that Una's illness was pivotal in altering
the relationship between Rose and her father. Because the family's attention was focused of necessity on Una, little attention
was available for the other two children. Rose, so the researcher
believes, grew up feeling and believing that she was not as well
loved as Una by either her mother or her father.[15]

On the other hand, seeing how well and lovingly her parents
nursed Una might have influenced Rose's choice of a career in
later life. With her mother's insistence on helping the poor and
both parents' ability to devote themselves when needed to nursing, Rose might have formed an understanding and an appreciation for nursing as an acceptable life's work.

In Search of a Religion

As adults, both Una and Rose Hawthorne chose to follow
different pathways than those of their parents. In the process,
both made unusual and unexpected choices in terms of lifestyle
and religious affiliation: Una as an Anglican and volunteer with
orphans, Rose as a nurse caring for cancer victims and in time as
a Catholic nun and founder of an order.

In some ways, Una and Rose's choices might be called a
return to the religious fervor that sparked the Hawthorne family through four generations. For the Puritan Hathornes, the religious impulse took the form of bigotry, a harsh conviction that

the Puritan expression of religion was the only correct one. Anyone not in sympathy, like the Quakers or the people accused of witchcraft in Salem in 1692, deserved persecution.

In Nathaniel, whose ties to organized religion were tenuous, the religious impulse took expression in his powerful writing and in the intense compassion he felt for fellow humans, especially those in trouble. The themes of the Puritan religion he learned as a youth – sin, evil, redemption – were reworked and transformed, appearing again and again in his sensitive psychological novels and short stories. At times his writing reveals Hawthorne's conviction that human beings are tied closely together; what affects one person is going to affect others, one way or another. A much-repeated story about Nathaniel's encounter as a consul in Liverpool with a boy deformed by leprosy and living in an alms home illustrates this. He wrote anonymously of the experience first in *Our Old Home*. Paraphrased, the encounter went like this: Nathaniel was touring the children's wing of an almshouse in Liverpool when he came upon a sad little boy suffering from leprosy. Sores covered his face. For some reason, the boy took to Nathaniel and stayed with him, rubbing against his legs and then raising his arms to be lifted up. A lover of beauty and fastidious to a point, a man who kept himself removed from the sordid side of life, from its messiness and distasteful side, Nathaniel found himself unexpectedly moved by pity when the sickly urchin made his appeal. Nathaniel lifted him up in his arms and held him.

In relating the experience, Nathaniel wrote how the emotion of the moment seized him, making him understand what it meant to be a human being – someone capable of responding to the great need of another. This was life's greatest opportunity, the writer indicated.

> It might almost make a man doubt the existence of his own soul, to observe how nature has flung these little wretches into the street and left them there. . . . Ah what a mystery! Slowly, slowly, as after groping at the bottom of a deep, noi-

some stagnant pool, my home struggles upward to the sur-
face, bearing the half-drowned body of a child along with
it, and heaving it aloft for its life, and my own life, and all
our lives. Unless these slime-clogged nostrils can be made
capable of inhaling celestial air, I know not how the purest
and most intellectual of us can reasonably expect ever to
taste a breath of it. The whole question of eternity is staked
there. If a single one of these helpless little ones is lost, the
whole world is lost.[16]

In the lives of Hawthorne's daughters, the religious impulse
gradually was transmuted into new religious affiliations that
gradually led them into new lives of service to society's out-
casts. Rejecting the lack of ties to organized religion favored by
their parents. Una became an Anglican in Britain and, apparently, was considering joining an Anglican order of religious sisters
at the time of her death in her early thirties.[17]

Rose converted to Roman Catholicism and, in time, founded
a religious order to better carry out her vocation of nursing destitute cancer patients. That religious order continues Rose's
work today.

In terms of how and why Rose and Una choose to convert
away from the Unitarianism of their early years, the records are
scanty. Neither sister left any extensive written record on why
they converted, or why they were attracted to their vocational
choices. Some conclusions about Rose's choices are documented
through her own writing, through her numerous letters and
through "Christ's Poor," the publication she founded to com-
municate news of her homes for patients and to support them.
Una's choices are documented only through the writing of other
family members such as her brother Julian.

Una and Rose both converted to religions that were considerably more structured than the Unitarian faith of their childhood. A possible reason for their choices might lie in the lack of
structure that they experienced as children. Nathaniel moved
his family frequently; they seldom lived in the same house for
an extended period of time, where they could put down roots

and develop a close network of friends and relations. Rose, for example, apparently had few, if any, close friendships outside the family as a youngster, youth, and as a young adult.

The Hawthorne children's lives became more difficult, especially financially, after Nathaniel's death in Plymouth, New Hampshire, in 1864. Initially, Sophia Hawthorne struggled to maintain her family in their home, "the Wayside." To assist the family financially, Sophia (the first of several relatives to do so) sought to build on Nathaniel's popularity as a foremost U.S. author by editing new versions or first publications of his writings. In the process she "cleansed" her husband's texts in journals and letters of any comments she judged would reflect poorly on him. Her intention was to preserve his memory as a larger-than-life figure, one to whom the ordinary foibles and faults of life did not apply.

Much of the first two years after Nathaniel's death, Sophia and Rose spent in each other's company as Una and Julian frequently were away from home. Julian left the family, to attend Harvard University. Una's fragile health meant she was away on trips to recuperate frequently. She was seriously ill in 1861 to 1862, for instance. And her first foray into love ended abruptly when her engagement to Storrow Higginson was broken by him. As a result, Una's none too steady emotional balance deteriorated.

Traveling for one's health was a favored way to help patients recover in the 19th century. Different scenes and climates were thought to exert a healing influence. Sophia herself traveled off and on for her health during her youth and early adulthood; she suffered from what probably were debilitating migraines.

The result was that in a few short years, Rose either lost entirely or was deprived of the presence for long stretches of family members she loved and relied on. In an 1867 letter to Una, Rose gave some idea of her feelings, calling her life "nothing but torment. I never shall have that rare pleasure of being loved infinitely, that is what makes a person the noblest and highest they dream of."[18]

In another letter to Una (July 15, 1866), Rose's comments suggested that she was placing her mother on a pedestal of perfection similar to that of her father. Rose compared herself unfavorably to either parent, convinced apparently that she could not possibly reach either her father's level of intellectual power or either parent's level of exalted virtue. Speaking of her mother, Rose wrote to Una:

> Just because heaven does not choose that I should be a genius, I am miserable and sour. . . . I know what I should do, but I don't, and I say, can't. I know that life is a wonderful chance – not to be wasted and lost but earned. . . . I think that a person should devote himself to others, forgetting himself, not thinking that he must perfect himself, and as he helps others to be good, he suddenly finds himself good. . . . I see how good Mama is; but it don't make me good.[19]

Adding to Rose's discontent was being sent to boarding school for the first time. By calling on the generous support of relatives such as a Cousin Mary and friends such as the Fields, Sophia was able to enroll Rose in two private schools for brief periods of time. One was a boarding school in Lexington, Massachusetts, for the fall semester in 1866.

From the first, however, Rose did not adjust well to boarding school life. She took an immediate dislike to her roommate and intensely disliked the regulated life of the school. In a letter to her mother, she begged her to send a letter to excuse her from obligatory chapel attendance. Unused to formal religious services, Rose hated the school's policy of compulsory attendance. Sophia refused.

Another sore point for Rose was her lack of spending money, especially for clothes and entertainments such as concerts. Rose loved clothes and pretty things, and felt herself very different from most girls in a school that catered mainly to the daughters of wealthy families. Sophia did what she could to provide money and clothes, but was forced by her circumstances to keep a tight grip on the purse strings.[20]

In time, Sophia concluded that she could not support her family adequately by staying in the United States. Accordingly, she sold the Wayside and in 1868 transported her family to Europe, to the city of Dresden. Sophia believed that the cultural and educational opportunities were more plentiful in Dresden, along with a lower cost of living. In Dresden, Rose studied art and Julian, now a Harvard grad and somewhat uncertain of his future, pursued engineering studies.

To learn the ways of their adopted home city, the Hawthornes soon became active in the city's social life with other American expatriates. Both Una and Rose, following the customary path of young women, took an interest in the city's available bachelors. Una eventually became engaged again, once again choosing unwisely. Her second fiancé, a tubercular poet, was ill and died while traveling in hopes of recovering his health.

Along with the rest of her family, Rose renewed her acquaintance with the Lathrop family, an American family the Hawthornes met initially in Liverpool. Along with the mother, the Lathrop family included two sons, George, who later became a journalist and editor, and Francis, who became a somewhat successful U.S. painter.[21]

After three years in Dresden, having discovered the cost of living higher than anticipated, Sophia moved once again, this time to England. In England, however, the country's damp cold weather served once again to Sophia's disadvantage. She became seriously ill. During this illness, her last, Una nursed her mother constantly, almost alone, in much the same way her mother and father once nursed her. For her part, Rose responded to her mother's final illness poorly. An incident related at a later time told how Rose became "hysterical and frightened" when she entered Sophia's sick room[22]) Sophia died on March 4, 1871, when Rose was barely twenty and Julian twenty five. Sophia was buried the day before Una's twenty-seventh birthday.

At the time of Sophia's death, Julian, an engineer, was living in New York. With the twin responsibilities of his work and concern about his pregnant wife, Minnie, Julian could not take the time to travel to England to bring his sisters back home. Accordingly, he asked his "kindred spirit" from Dresden, George Lathrop, to travel to England and escort his sisters back across the ocean.[23]

However, that request resulted in a breach between Julian and George Lathrop, laying the groundwork for Julian's lifelong disdain for George. It also caused a rift in the relationship between Rose and her brother and sister.

Shortly after George Lathrop arrived in England, he and Rose became engaged. Though George and the three Hawthornes had been friends, and even though there was some evidence that George and Rose took more than a casual interest in each other, the couple's plan to marry dismayed and shocked most of the Hawthorne family. And there was good reason for objection: The couple was young, George was nineteen and Rose barely twenty, on their wedding day in September 1871 at St. Luke's Anglican Church in Chelsea. No Hawthorne family members were present, only George's brother.

In addition, neither Rose or George had a sufficient source of income, or even an established idea of a vocation. Then too, the couple married just six months after Sophia Hawthorne's death, before the usual time of mourning had ended.[24] Looked at from today's perspective of the stages of the grieving process, it is possible to conclude that Rose married hastily, before truly grieving for her mother and adjusting to the new circumstance of being bereft of both beloved parents.

On hearing news of the engagement, Una also reacted with displeasure and refused to attend her sister's wedding. Within two days Una had lapsed into a depression severe enough to require a stay in an asylum. Ten years earlier, Una had suffered through her first serious bout of what proved to be recurring mental illness; she was institutionalized at the time and given electric shock treatments.

One researcher suggested that Una's disapproval of her sister's marriage to George Lathrop may have been based largely on the recognition that she henceforth truly was on her own. Her parents were dead, she was unmarried, and her brother was a family man, intent on supporting his wife and children.[25] On the other hand, since Una periodically suffered from fragile mental health, there is no way to say for sure why she responded to her sister's wedding as she did.

Julian, on the other hand, later referred to his sister's marriage by remarking that it was "an error, not to be repaired."[26] A biographer suggests Julian might have thought that George Lathrop had taken advantage of his request to escort Rose and Una to the United States.

In time Una recovered from her second serious mental illness. She then worked with Robert Browning on the publication of Nathaniel's book, *Septimius Felton*, while refusing to restore relationships with her sister. Ultimately Una moved to England, and occupied herself with doing volunteer settlement work at a home for orphans run by Anglicans. She had been confirmed into Anglicanism in 1869, but what led her to make this choice is unclear.

In late 1871, George and Rose Lathrop left England to return to the United States. Initially they lived with George's mother for six months in New York City's Greenwich Village. After trying and abandoning plans to study law, George had settled on a writing career, which he pursued with some success. Drawing on the power of Nathaniel's fame, he wrote an article called "History of Hawthorne's Last Romance" to accompany Una's publication of *Septimius Felton*. The *Atlantic Monthly* published the article in 1872. George also began to write poetry and fiction, and soon began to appear regularly in New York City journals and magazines. His success led to him becoming an associate editor at the *Atlantic Monthly*, the first source of steady income for the young couple. He and Rose became respected members of the New York intellectual and journalistic world.[27]

Rose, too, tried her hand at writing short stories and poems. However, she never achieved the success as a writer that her father or even her husband had. She too worked on Nathaniel Hawthorne material, publishing a book, *Memories of Hawthorne* in 1895.

Adding to the lack of stability in Rose's life, from the start, she and George experienced difficulties in their marriage; this resulted in several separations over the years. They had sufficient reason too: In common with Rose's parents, the couple seldom knew financial security. At times they were almost destitute, surviving for a time on the donations of friends.

According to family reports, Rose, a beautiful and impulsive redhead, probably was not easy to live with; she had a temper to match her hair. This dates back to her childhood, for one of her father's letters to Rose refers in a lighthearted way to her sometimes unruly behavior.

George suffered on and off from an unspecified gastric disorder, which finally led to a period during which the doctors refused to let him work; this made the couple's financial status bleak indeed. His gastric disorder ultimately led to his hospitalization and death in 1898. Researchers make various suggestions on what George's illness was. Some suggest he had an ongoing battle with alcoholism. Others hint that he was abusive to Rose, possibly while drinking, and this led to their several separations.

As the years passed, the couple's financial situation did not improve. Convinced that the excitement and frequent parties of cosmopolitan New York City exacerbated George's physical condition, Rose in time decided that the solution was to move to a quieter location. And, in 1879, she and George purchased her old family home, the Wayside, and moved there to live. This period provided a respite from the wanderings and unsettledness of the couple's usual existence. This respite ended, however, with the death of their only son, Francis (born in 1876), before the age of six. This provoked Rose into a prolonged bout of melancholy that began to lift only when George sold the Wayside and the couple moved away from the home with its painful memories. Her condition at this point was less serious than the severe "puerperal insanity" (today it would be called "postpartum psychosis or depression") Rose experienced following Francis's birth in 1876; this resulted in her being hospitalized at McLean Asylum for the Insane to recover. She left the asylum in the early months of 1877.[28]

In time, the young couple decided to explore a new religion together that was neither Rose's nominal Unitarianism nor George's Episcopalianism. The outcome was that in 1891 Paulist Father James Young baptized Rose and George Lathrop into the Catholic Church in New York City. As the couple's spiritual advisor, Young had conducted Rose and George's education in the mysteries and doctrines of Catholicism.[29]

Because of the couple's prominence in the literary world and Rose's status as the daughter of Nathaniel, the news of the couple's conversion to Catholicism raised a ruckus in the secular press and the Catholic press. The Catholic press rejoiced in snaring such prominent converts. Much of the secular press was scornful, partly because there still was considerable anti-Catholic feeling in the country and partly because Catholicism of the late 1800s was identified as a religion of immigrants, of a lower class.[30]

In response to the uproar, George Lathrop wrote an article explaining his decision to become Catholic that was published in the New York *Independent*, a newspaper that had condemned his conversion. Here he emphasized that "Christianity was not belated study," given his and Rose's prior religious interests. In defending his choice, George centered on Catholicism's rational approach to faith. He spoke of

> reason as an essential groundwork of belief . . . while Protestantism was preeminently a matter of the heart and sundry vague leadings of the spirit and that between reason and belief there is a gap which can be crossed only by using a sort of leaping-pole of unquestioning, unreasoning belief.[31]

Rose did not write a similar apologia for becoming Catholic. (One biographer states that Rose had her son baptized a Roman Catholic in Boston in 1876; this has not been verified, however.) Later Rose indicated that her first inclination might have been toward another religion. She tells how she and her husband had reached the point of realizing that they "were not happy about religion. We saw we had need of it and one day I told him that I thought that some Presbyterian friends of ours seemed to derive benefit from their faith." She goes on to explain that George's reply was, "If I ever change, the only church I'll ever join is the Catholic Church."[32]

Though all their reasons for converting to Catholicism cannot be stated, one striking fact is that the milieu around them was one of intellectual ferment and even restlessness. This reflected the larger society as well. People of intellect and education discussed religious and spiritual ideas and often experimented with different forms of religion before accepting one to join or deciding to remain aloof. It was not considered unacceptable to change religions, perhaps even several times, as did Isaac Hecker, who later converted to Catholicism and founded the Paulist Fathers. The Paulist Fathers' main focus was in what today is called "social justice" matters and in reaching out to people beyond the Catholic Church. The Paulists were pioneers in presenting an open face to people who were not Catholics.

Another factor might have been the popularity of conversion in the 19th century. A researcher points out that conversions in the late 19th century were common, even fashionable, whether to Catholicism or one of the various Protestant denominations. Also intellectuals discussed the need to be involved in activities aimed at changing the basic structures of society in order to better the society around them and improve the lives of those who had no one to act as their advocate. The Paulist Fathers were among the leaders of this approach. (A Paulist priest instructed Rose and George in the Catholic faith, thus giving them first-hand information about Paulist philosophy of life.)

Statistics from the century indicate that the Catholic population in the United States was undergoing great expansion. In 1880 there were six million Catholics in the United States; by 1910 there were 16 million Catholics in the United States.[33] Much of the increase, but not all, can be traced to births and especially to the vast number of European immigrants who came to the United States in the mid- to latter 19th century.

Speculations

Perhaps, given the unstable character of her entire life to date, Rose as well as her husband may have found Catholicism attractive precisely because it was a highly structured religion with definite dogmas and tradition. Catholicism also has a tradition of superb liturgical practices full of pageantry and music and color. Catholicism had the ability to appeal to people's hearts as well as their minds. Perhaps this appealed to a couple whose life was somewhat lacking in permanent roots.

Rose, especially, seldom knew a permanent home and therefore was not blessed with a wide network of close friends with a long history of shared experiences. Throughout her childhood and then as a young wife and mother, Rose moved frequently, seldom staying in the same home for more than a couple of years at a time.

Only after she moved to Rosary Hill did Rose find a permanent home – one she stayed in for thirty-some years. And it was only after she started her life's work as a nurse that she made what became the longest lasting and most nourishing friendship of her life with the co-founder of her order, Alice Huber.

In addition, as a married couple, the Lathrops had a number of friends who were Catholic, including some who converted to Catholicism, such as Alfred and Adelaide Chappell. The Lathrops went to Catholic services with the Chappells and borrowed books to deepen their knowledge of Catholicism from them as well. They also had a Catholic servant, Nellie Sullivan, who remained Rose's friend after she married and left her service.

For Rose, another factor may have been the desolation she felt at the many deaths she endured, starting with those of her mother and father. Then in the space of a single year, three people close to Rose died – her son Francis, her sister Una, and her Aunt Elizabeth Hawthorne. In an interview for *Ladies Home Journal*, Rose said that her son's death "made the next world more real than this." With its firm belief in resurrection and an after life, Catholicism might well have had a special appeal for Rose.

Following their conversion, Rose and George threw themselves wholeheartedly into Catholic causes and soon won a place among leading Catholic intellectuals and writers. She and George joined the lecture circuit. Soon Rose was in demand for her lectures in Catholic circles and schools on social justice causes, such as Catholic Charities and their beneficial work with the poor. This is another sign of Rose's growing interest in social justice causes and in being of service to society. Abandoning her efforts to place poetry and romantic short stories, Rose focused on various social justice issues.

In Search of a Life's Work

Rose, like her sister Una, chose to dedicate her life in a far from customary way. At the age of forty five, Rose turned away from a comfortable life of relative leisure that included associating with the leading intellectual and artistic people in society to embrace the unrelenting work of nursing dying and impoverished cancer victims, patients most people shunned. Subsequently she affiliated with the Dominican Order and became the founder and mother superior as Mother Alphonsa of a religious order of nuns, the Servants of Relief for Incurable Cancer.

Yet, in some ways, neither sister's choice of life work was so surprising, given the Hawthorne family tradition. On the mother's side of the family, there is a considerable history of Peabody women pursuing careers and activities aimed at improving the world around them.

The three Peabody sisters as young women were at the hub of Boston intellectual life. While Sophia chose to devote her energies to the life of a wife and mother, she always kept an interested eye on the intellectual trends of the day. Her two sisters pursued active careers outside the home through most of their lives.

All three Peabody sisters, perhaps repeating the pattern of their mother who periodically conducted a school for youths from her home, set a pattern of strong, resourceful, independent women willing to take risks for their causes. They also showed great willingness to switch gears when the need was at hand, turning from one vocation to another either because of their changing interests or because of financial necessity.

Sophia, a skilled artist and copyist, produced copies of famous painters' works that then were sold to people who could not afford the originals. She used this avocation to help support herself before her marriage and also after her marriage to raise money on occasion when Nathaniel's fortunes were at a low point. She also successfully edited her husband's works to support her family after his death.

Mary, as the wife of Horace Mann, the founder of the American school system, worked hand in glove with her husband as an educational reformer. In addition she raised their children.

In the course of a long life as a single woman (she died at

almost ninety), Elizabeth Peabody tried her hand at several different careers. She is credited with opening the first woman-owned bookstore in Boston, with financial help from Channing. She also became the first woman publisher (including publishing Hawthorne's *Twicetold Tales*).[34] Her main success came in her late fifties, when she led the battle to establish kindergartens in the United States educational systems and also schools to educate teachers for the kindergartens. A biographer reports that Elizabeth was much admired for turning down a suitor and turning resolutely away from a life of ease to do good in the world.[35]

Rose's choice of a vocation, though not in the same field, mirrored that of her Aunt Elizabeth Peabody in some interesting ways. Elizabeth may well have been Rose's model in setting out resolutely down a difficult path in the face of skepticism and doubt. Among her many talents, Elizabeth was a master at fundraising, for her own causes as well as the causes of people she believed in. One such was the cause of Princess Winnemucca, a Piute Native American whom Peabody helped support through written appeals for money for six months.[36]

In later years and perhaps remembering her aunt's fundraising successes, whenever Rose needed to raise money to support her nursing homes for her cancer patients, she fired off letters of appeal to the newspapers. The newspapers, because of her reputation as the daughter of one of America's greatest literary figures and also because she and her husband both had labored in the literary field and earned a reputation, responded favorably with space in the newspapers.

As her Peabody aunt had done, Rose also sold tickets to lecture series to raise funds. In time, she developed a devoted group of physicians and others who were consistent and reliable benefactors to her work. Her Aunt Elizabeth did the same, selling subscriptions to lecture series to raise funds for a school she and Bronson Alcott were founding.

A contributing factor for Rose's vocation choice might be the experience she and George had in writing the history of the

Visitation order in 1892–93. Published in 1894 as *A Story of Courage*, the book tells the story of the Visitation's founder, St. Jane de Chantal, along with the history of the academy's founding. It is possible that Rose found herself identifying closely with the life of St. Jane.

Jane de Chantal was a widow and a mother and a woman who was hungry for the religious life and for finding a cause to devote herself to, especially a cause that helped the poor. In time she became the founder of a religious community devoted to teaching poor girls.

While researching the book for the Visitation sisters, the Lathrops lived in close proximity to the sisters in Washington, D.C., which gave them good insight to the life the nuns led. In their introduction to the history, the Lathrops speak in the warmest tones of the nuns' life, of its purity and goodness and happiness. Rose is now credited as being the primary author of the history, as George's health at the time was deteriorating.

By the time Rose became a Catholic at the age of forty, she had experienced a full measure of loss including several separations from her husband and the deaths of people most dear to her. This included the death of her friend, Emma Lazarus, a wealthy Jewess who is remembered for her work with Jewish immigrants and for her poem welcoming immigrants to the United States that is carved on the Statue of Liberty.

After several short-term separations, Rose left George permanently in 1895 and received a church-approved separation in 1896.[37] George, refusing to accept her decision as final, insisted that "I have kept the path open" to resuming married life. Rose, however, refused adamantly. She wrote in an 1895 letter to a friend, "It was not without years of prayer and thought and patience and weighing wise counsel, that I have taken the step I have in leaving my husband's care forever. His pain now in the separation is very sad. I doubt that it is greater than the long pain I have suffered and ever more suffer."[38]

Rose was indignant when George suggested that her choice of a vocation was a sign that the mental breakdown she had experienced many years previously had returned. George wrote Rose that he thought her best hope for recovery "lies in your putting yourself under thorough and special medical care for the restoration of your nervous system." In response, Rose replied that he "would prefer to have me in a mental asylum than working for charity!"

However, despite her insistence on living apart from her husband, several years later, upon receiving word that George was dying in 1898 – according to the state death certificate, of chronic nephritis, a recurrent kidney disease – Rose hurried to his bedside at the New York hospital and was distressed to find him already dead. Much shocked at his (to her) unexpected death, Rose shortly afterwards referred to him as "my beloved husband" in writing about his death.[39] A major part of her dismay appears to be grounded in the fact that George died before she could convince him of the value of her work as a nurse.[40] Two days after his death, Rose told how she found consolation. She said that during her sleep she saw George's soul coming "to console me, in his loveliest way of forgiveness." She later writes to a friend of her conviction that George approves of her work: "Now I feel sure that he is in accord with me, and praying for the success of this charity."[41]

Once Rose separated permanently from her husband, it took her little time to determine what to do. She made a retreat with the Sisters of Charity in Wellesley Hills, Massachusetts, based on the life and works of St. Vincent de Paul. This would have given Rose information on how Vincent had founded a series of headquarters or stores where poor people and those down on their luck could come to buy second-hand clothes and goods at affordable prices.

Shortly after the retreat, Rose enrolled in a three-month nursing course at Memorial Hospital in New York City to learn how to care for cancer patients. This took heroism, since much of the work involved constantly removing and dressing the cancer sores on the patient's body. Cancer at the time was a disfiguring disease, and many people shrank from cleaning such wounds.

Cancer in the late 19th century was viewed with the same sort of horror and fear that leprosy once was. People thought cancer was contagious, and, in the case of those without family and/or funds, those fears led them to abandon those in great need who were penniless.

In the custom of the day, once patients were declared incurable, they were forced to leave the hospital. For poor patients, the result was disastrous – often it meant a lonely trip to Blackwell's Island to die in isolation and degradation and misery. Comparing poor patients' fate with that of her friend, Emma Lazarus, who died in the midst of a loving and wealthy family, showed Rose how stark a contrast there was between those with funds and those without.

In 1896, Rose turned away forever from her previous life. She left upper New York, the city of the rich and respectable, of large homes and expensive stores and went into the New York of the lower East side, a slum area where the streets were crowded and the houses dingy and the people neither rich nor respected. Determined to live in the same area and in the same way as the female cancer patients she would nurse, Rose chose an apartment at 1 Scammel Street. At the top of a frame house, on a noisy street not far from the East River, the apartment had three tiny rooms with filthy windows looking out onto an alley. Rose wanted destitute cancer patients to live out their last days in homey and comfortable surroundings. Therefore she scrubbed and cleaned the apartment and then painted its three rooms; she painted the walls a pure white and the floors a bright yellow.

When the apartment was ready, Rose determined to invite a cancer patient to become her first permanent guest. One day she received a note written by a Mrs. Watson, the first cancer patient Rose treated while in nursing training. After describing how her illness had deteriorated, Mrs. Watson asked Rose, "Can I come and stay with you?" A grandmother, Mrs. Watson's suffered from a particularly disfiguring skin cancer. And so Mrs. Watson became Rose's first "permanent guest."

In turning her apartment into a home for dying cancer patients, it might be fitting to compare Rose to the European founders of what is known today as the "hospice" movement. Founded initially in England, the hospice movement sought to provide dying patients with the means to live out their last days at home, surrounded by family and other people's loving care, rather than in a sterile hospital with strangers as nurses. Somewhat similarly but with her own unique stamp, Rose created a "home away from home" for cancer victims who had nowhere else to go. Rose's long-range dream was to establish an institution for dying cancer patients without means. Initially Rose treated women patients only; in time, however, she was able to extend her care to men as well, when she opened larger quarters.

With Mrs. Watson moved into her Scammel Street apartment, Rose was well launched on realizing her dream of caring for the most pitiable cancer patients. It also was a crucial step in a journey that led the daughter of the Puritan Hawthornes to a cause worthy of her talents, one that consumed her mind and heart along with her considerable talents and organizational ability.

Rose's newfound cause also provided her the most stable home she had ever had and a close companionship with the women who joined her over the years, most particularly, Alice Huber, who became her first companion and coworker in 1897. In pursuing her vision, Rose Hawthorne found the fulfillment that had long eluded her, content in doing what she believed God had called her to do.

Rose on her Vocation

Asked to explain in her old age why she chose the life's work she did, Rose said that the strongest influence was her father and the sympathy he consistently showed for those captured by poverty and disease. She referred often to the story of the ragged little orphan Hawthorne encountered in a workhouse during his European travels, an instance when he realized what it meant to be a human being – someone capable of responding to the great need of another. This was life's greatest opportunity, the writer indicated.

In commenting on the story, Rose explained how touched she was. She also would have been aware of her father's generosity toward destitute sailors while he served as consul. One reason he returned to the United States with less of a financial nest egg than he had expected is because he was unwilling to say no when a sailor approached him for funds.

Throughout her three decades as a nurse, Rose returns again and again to the topic of why she chose such an out-of-the-ordinary life's work. She offered a variety of explanations. A primary reason is her strong desire to be useful. Her brother Julian reported that "the leaven had long been working in her." This seems to be borne out by an 1869 letter Rose wrote from Dresden, Germany. In it she said she needed "an excuse for being in the world.

Rose provided a lengthy explanation of her choice in an article published in *Ainslee's Magazine* in 1898. *Ainslee's* editor's introductions states that the magazine "is honored in being the medium by which Mrs. Rose Hawthorne Lathrop was making an appeal to the whole people of the United States for interest in the Christ-like labor and charity to which she has consecrated her life."

In the article, Rose wrote:

> I have always been sorry for the poor, in which I resemble most people, no doubt, and I have tried all my life to express this pity in some practical usefulness. . . . Having the chance to devote myself to what is called charity, I seized upon it, and chose a field which I saw was neglected in this country (though not in France and England). I chose the field of nursing destitute women suffering from cancer, and kindred diseases."[42]

At the time Rose wrote that article, she had succeeded in recruiting three like-minded women to help her and together the four were caring for six patients. Rose also had moved to larger quarters at 668 Water Street.

In explaining why she was bringing her cause before the public, Rose states in the *Ainslee* article: "My hope is to bring the need into the light and before the public so constantly and thoroughly that a dignified development will be hastened and a permanent life for it ensured." Rose then appeals to the public for donations to help support her home and establish larger quarters. She directs a special invitation to women "who are capable of giving up whatever is sweet in personal freedom or delicious in physical ease (to) think seriously of adding themselves to this group of workers."

Another reason why Rose is willing to take up such a difficult vocation can be traced to grief in losing her only child. Shortly after her son's death, Rose wrote a friend, "A married woman, loving children as I do and bereft of them, must, it seems to me, fill the void in her life with works of charity."

In one of her last letters before her death at seventy five, Rose says, "I never really wanted to write about life. I wanted to live it."

Perhaps the best summary of why she had dedicated her life to such a demanding vocation came in an article Rose wrote in the *Christian Herald*:

> I am trying to serve the poor as a servant. I wish to serve the cancerous poor because they are avoided more than any other class of sufferers; and I wish to go to them as a poor creature myself, though powerful to help them through the open-handed gifts of public kindness, because it is by humility and sacrifice alone that we feel the holy spirit of pity.

In the first years of the 21st century, the Roman Catholic Church has started proceedings into naming Rose Hawthorne Lathrop as a possible saint.

Endnotes

1   Rose Hawthorne Lathrop, *Memories of Hawthorne* (Boston: Houghton Mifflin Co., 1923), pp.70–75.

2   Patricia Dunlavy Valenti, *To Myself a Stranger: A Biography of Rose Hawthorne Lathrop* (Baton Rouge: Louisiana State University Press, 1991), p. 1.

3   Lathrop, p. 151

4   *Ibid*, p. 212.

5   *Ibid*, pp. 214–17; 297–98.

6   *Ibid.*, p. 244.

7   Julian Hawthorne, *Hawthorne and His Wife*, pp. 138–40.

8   Lathrop, pp. 192, 54.

9   T. Walter Herbert, *Dearest Beloved: The Hawthornes and the Making of the Middle Class Family* (Berkeley: University of California Press, 1993), p. 110.

10   Valenti, p. 31.

11   *The Marble Faun* from *Novels* (The Library of America, 1983), p. 1100.

12   Lathrop, p. 460.

13   *The Marble Faun*, pp. 1154–55.

14   Julian Hawthorne, *Hawthorne and His Wife*, II, p. 324.

15   Margaret Kahn, "Rose of the Hawthorne," unpublished article.

16   Nathaniel Hawthorne, *Our Old Home: A Series of English Sketches*, The Centenary Edition (Columbus: Ohio State University Press, 1972).

17   Julian Hawthorne, *Hawthorne and His Wife*, II, p. 324.

18   Quoted in Valenti, RH letter dated Dec. 13, 1865, in Berg Collection.

19   Valenti, p. 33.

20   *Ibid.*, p. 35.

21   *Ibid.*, pp. 40–43.

22   Julian Hawthorne, *Hawthorne and His Wife*, II, pp. 361, 366.

23   Valenti, pp. 43–44, 48.

24   *Ibid.*, pp. 47–48.

25   *Ibid.*, p. 50.

26   *Ibid.*, p. 48.

27   *Ibid.*, pp. 51–52.

28   *Ibid.*, pp. 57–58.

29   A spokesman for the Paulist priests in Washington, D.C., told the authors that no records are extant concerning the couple's initiation into Catholicism.

30   Valenti, p. 100.

31   *Ibid.*, p. 101.

32   *Ibid*, p. 102

33   Diane Culbertson, "Rose Hawthorne Lathrop: Selected Writings of Mother Alphonsa, Founder of the Servants of Relief for Incurable Cancer," *Sources of American Spirituality* (Mahwah, N.J.: Paulist Press, 1993).

34   Louise Hall Tharp, *The Peabody Sisters of Salem* (London: George G. Harrap and Co., 1951; Boston: Little, Brown and Co., 1988), p. 122.

35   *Ibid.*, p. 36.

36   *Ibid.*, p. 282.

37   Valenti, p. 128.

38   *Ibid.*, p. 127.

39   *Ibid.*, p. 147.

40   *Ibid.*, p. 130.

41   *Ibid.*, p. 148.

42   *Ainslee's Magazine*, April 1898, pp. 49–51.

Epilogue

From 1926 to today is a long time to remember, especially in the United States where memories often are short. Yet the remarkable achievements of the Hawthorne family continue to call forth the exercise of memory. For the earliest Puritan Hawthornes, the exercise leads to Salem and the Salem witch trials. For Nathaniel Hawthorne, the author, the exercise begins with a visit to the nearest library or bookstore. For Rose Hawthorne Lathrop, the exercise is best accomplished by a pilgrimage to Hawthorne, New York.

In Hawthorne is Rosary Hill, Rose Hawthorne Lathrop's final and most permanent home. Located on a hillside on broad sweeping lawns filled in the Spring with the lovely blooms of tulips and dogwood, magnolia and lilac trees, Rosary Hill is the latest reincarnation of the home founded by Rose in 1901 to house her dying cancer patients. Built in the mid-1980s of sandstone topped by red tiles in the Spanish mansion style, Rosary Hill is a fitting memorial to the memory of Rose Hawthorne, a daughter of Nathaniel in whom religious fervor and sensitivity, compassion and practicality and a sense of duty were entwined.

Rosary Hill is an extended care facility for cancer patients with no financial means. The home, true to Rose Hawthorne Lathrop's mandate, accepts no patients with financial means. If they can afford to pay, they go elsewhere. The home accepts no government funds and is supported out of the legacies people have donated over the years to the home.

The fifty men and women who come here are admitted only after medicine and surgery have done their best. The average patient lives about three months; six months is a long time; two years exceptional.[1] Rosary Hill's atmosphere is cheerful and hospitable; each room has a sweeping window looking over the beautiful countryside. The home is immaculate, with flower pots lining corridors and a solarium where patients can go to sit in wicker furniture to enjoy the sun, talk with visitors or play the piano.

Throughout, the home carries out Rose Lathrop's determination that, since her patients are "coming home to die," they should have a place to come that is "simple as a country farm house, and fresh and cheery."[2] Much of the home's atmosphere is generated by the nurses, aides, and volunteers who care for Rosary Hill's patients. Many are members of the Hawthorne Dominicans, the religious community of women Rose Hawthorne Lathrop founded to help in her work of mercy and compassion.

Those in search of Hawthorne family memories might visit the "shrine" of memorabilia in a small room in Rosary Hill. This contains photographs, a locket containing a lock of Rose Hawthorne Lathrop's son Francis, and her many daily journals and letters that provide an invaluable record to the daily life and difficulties faced by Rose in establishing her homes. Another room to visit is Rosary Hill's chapel, the chapel built for an earlier Rosary Hill whose foundation stone she set in place in June 1926, shortly before her death. A bronze tablet set in a wall by the home's front door and written by Alice Huber, Rose Hawthorne Lathrop's companion in work (and the person she called "my first born in this enterprise of burning love for Lord"), states: "We who have completed this home must bear in mind that she who laid the foundation stone braved many hardships and difficulties. We have only finished what she commenced and made secure. May her name be held in everlasting remembrance."

A letter written by Alice Huber to her sister Annie (August 13, 1899)[3] reveals that the altar's origins go back even further, to the Water Street home for cancer patients in New York City. In this letter, Huber writes that they are installing a new altar into their little chapel, adding that it is "Mrs. Lathrop's gift, bought out of money left to her by her father," Nathaniel. Huber adds, "I don't imagine Hawthorne ever expected any of his money would be spent on Catholic altars."

Endnotes

1　Interview with Mother Bernadette, April 1991.

2　Newspaper appeal by Lathrop asking for funds Feb. 1899, in *Christ's Poor*, 1, no. 2.

3　Undated letter, *letters*, vol. 1.

Bibliography

Aquinas, Thomas, *Summa Theologica*.

Blackstone, William, *Commentaries on the Laws of England*, edited by George Sharswood, 2 vols. (Philadelphia: J. B. Lippincott & Co., 1872).

"Body of Liberties," in *Massachusetts Historical Society Collections*, VIII: 216-37.

The Book of Common Prayer (New York: Oxford University Press, 1929).

"The Cambridge Platform," in *American Christianity*, Vol I, pp. 129-40.

Channing, William E., "Unitarian Christianity," in *American Christianity*, Vol. I, pp. 493–502.

Culbertson, Diane, ed., "Rose Hawthorne Lathrop: Selected Writings of Mother Alphonsa, Founder of the Servants of Relief for Incurable Cancer," *Sources of American Spirituality* (Mahwah, N.J.: Paulist Press, 1993).

Felt, Joseph B., *Annals of Salem* (W & S B Ives, 1845).

Hawthorne, Julian, *Hawthorne and His Wife*, vol. II, 324. (Boston: Houghton-Mifflin, 1901).

Hawthorne, Nathaniel *Novels*, (The Library of America, 1983): *The Scarlet Letter* in *Novels*, pp. 115–345.

The House of the Seven Gables in Novels, pp. 347-627.

The Blithedale Romance in Novels, pp. 629-848.

The Marble Faun in Novels, pp. 849-1242.

Hawthorne, Nathaniel, *The American Notebooks*, The Centenary Edition, Vol. VIII (Columbus: Ohio State University Press, 1972).

Hawthorne, Nathaniel, *Our Old Home: A Series of English Sketches*, The Centenary Edition (Columbus: Ohio State University Press, 1972).

Hawthorne, Nathaniel, *Tales and Sketches* (The Library of America, 1982):

"Endicott and the Red Cross" in *Tales*, pp. 542-48.

"Fancy's Show Box" in *Tales*, pp. 450–55.

"The Snow-Image," Preface in *Tales*, pp. 1154–57.

"Egotism; or the Bosom-Serpent" in *Tales*, pp. 781–94.

"The Christmas Banquet" in *Tales*, pp. 849–67.

"Main Street" in *Tales*, pp. 1023–50.

"Alice Doane's Appeal" in *Tales*, pp. 205–16.

"Mrs. Hutchinson" in *Tales*, pp. 18–24.

"The May-Pole of Merry Mount" in *Tales*, pp. 360–70.

"The Hall of Fantasy" in *Tales*, pp. 734–45.

"The Celestial Rail-road" in *Tales*, pp. 808–24.

"The Man of Adamant" in *Tales*, pp. 421–28.

"Earth's Holocaust" in *Tales*, pp. 887–906.

"Young Goodman Brown" in *Tales*, pp. 276–89.

"The Gentle Boy" in *Tales*, pp. 108–38.

"Ethan Brand" in *Tales*, pp. 350–63.

"Mosses from an Old Manse," Preface in *Tales*, pp. 1123–53.

Hawthorne, Nathaniel, "John Davenport's Creed" in *American Christianity*, Vol. I, pp. 107–14.

Herbert, T. Walter: *Dearest Beloved: The Hawthornes and the Making of the Middle Class Family* (Berkeley: University of California Press, 1993).

Hutchinson, Thomas, *The History of the Colony and Province of Massachusetts Bay*, edited by L. S. Mayo (Cambridge, Mass.: Harvard University Press, 1936).

Joseph, Sr. Mary, *Out of Many Hearts* (New York: Servants of Relief for Incurable Cancer, 1965).

Juliana, Sr. M., "Rose Hawthorne's Unique Apostolate." Dominican Sisters of Hawthorne, reprint from *Immaculata* (Jan. 1976).

Kahn, Margaret, "Rose of the Hawthornes." Unpublished article, undated. _

Lathrop, Rose Hawthorne

Memories of Hawthorne (Boston: Houghton Mifflin Co., 1923).

Journals, Diaries and Memorabilia in Rosary Hill Archives, Hawthorne, N.Y. Reviewed by author in 1992.

Loggins, Vernon, *The Hawthornes: The Story of Seven Generations of an American Family* (New York: Columbia University Press, 1951).

Longfellow, H. W., *The Complete Poetical Works* (Boston: Houghton-Mifflin Company, undated).

Mather, Cotton, "Life of John Elliot," *Magnalia Christi Americana*, Book III in Miller and Johnson, Vol II (New York: Harper & Row, 1963)

Mather, Cotton, *The Wonders of the Invisible World* (London, 1862).

Maynard, Theodore, *A Fire Was Lighted: The Life of Rose Hawthorne Lathrop* (Milwaukee: Bruce Publishing Co., 1948).

Miller, E. H., *Salem Is My Dwelling Place: A Life of Nathaniel Hawthorne* (Iowa City: Iowa University Press, 1991).

Miller, Perry and Johnson, T. H., *The Puritans* (New York: Harper & Row, Publishers, 1963).

Smith, H. Shelton, Robert T. Handy, and Lefferts A. Loetscher, eds., *American Christianity: An Historical Interpretation with Representative Documents*, 2 vols. (New York: Charles Scribner's Sons, 1960).

Tharp, Louise Hall, *The Peabody Sisters of Salem* (London: George G. Harrap and Co., 1951; Boston: Little, Brown and Co., 1988).

Valenti, Patricia Dunlavy, *To Myself a Stranger: A Biography of Rose Hawthorne Lathrop* (Baton Rouge: Louisiana State University Press, 1991).

Walsh, James J. *Mother Alphonsa: Rose Hawthorne Lathrop* (New York: Macmillan Co., 1930).

Index